Praise for Sue Halpern's
Migrations to Solitude

"Powerful . . . thoughtful . . . Halpern's view of solitude is expansive, original and exploratory. . . . [She] is an uncommonly gifted and compassionate writer."

—Los Angeles Times

"In her modest and wise book, Sue Halpern takes the reader on an unusual journey across the country to look at what could be considered the other side of the coin of privacy, solitude."

—The New York Times

"Written with a light touch . . . [*Migrations to Solitude*] is about aloneness and privacy and the satisfactions people can find in being by themselves."

—The New Yorker

"Beautifully written . . . [Halpern] has a distinctive voice, a style that is impressionistic and suggestive, rather than routinely reportorial. This is as it should be, for to write about solitude is to write about people. We trust her implicitly."

—Los Angeles Daily News

"Moving . . . Sue Halpern has a beautifully delicate, deep prose style [and] in *Migrations to Solitude* . . . she helps us understand . . . the individual stories we each carry within ourselves."

—Seattle Times/Post-Intelligencer

"Halpern [has] a remarkable sensitivity to solitude's unexpected appearances, [and] a finely honed prose style. [She] is a vivid chronicler."

—*Newsday*

"Suggestive and gracefully written."

—*Village Voice Literary Supplement*

"Halpern . . . writes with an economical, eloquent style. The essays blend third-person descriptions with the writer's own impressions [which] are revealing, even poignant. . . . A reader who takes time away for this book should return the better for having done so."

—*San Diego Union-Tribune*

"Sue Halpern brilliantly uncovers the territory of privacy, of the individual alone in the world by choice or circumstance. [She] is sharp and observant, capturing both the idea and the reality of isolation with a voice so astute, so nearly perfect, it will break your heart."

—*L.A. Reader*

"Mixing meditation with reportage, these supple essays probe issues of solitude and privacy, and the ways we can choose or be forced or not be allowed to live alone."

—*Mirabella*

"An exploration of a series of characters and situations and their common theme of privacy, arrived at so variously and in each case, of course, as originally as all truly private things are. Indeed, originality, the meaning of it, is part of her subject, and her approach to it is compassionate, rounded, and lucidly conveyed, and a delight to read."

—W. S. Merwin

Sue Halpern
Migrations to Solitude

Sue Halpern holds a doctorate from Oxford University, where she was a Rhodes scholar. She has written for *The New York Review of Books*, *Rolling Stone*, the *New York Times*, *Antaeus*, *Sports Illustrated*, and *Granta*. She lives in the Adirondack Mountains of New York State with her husband and dog.

Migrations to Solitude

Sue Halpern

VINTAGE BOOKS

A DIVISION OF RANDOM HOUSE, INC.

NEW YORK

Library of Congress Cataloging-in-Publication Data

Halpern, Sue.
Migrations to solitude / Sue Halpern. — 1st Vintage Books ed.
p.   cm.
Originally published: New York: Pantheon Books, c1992
ISBN 0-679-74241-7
1. Privacy. 2. Solitude. I. Title.
[BF637.P74H35   1993]
155.9′2—dc20   92-56362
CIP

Book design and photography © Fearn Cutler

Author photograph © Bill McKibben

Manufactured in the United States of America
10 9 8 7 6 5

Contents

Author's Note   vii

Wild Ducks, People, & Distances   1

New Heaven and Earth   9

The Place of the Solitaries   33

A Room of One's Own   47

In Solitude, for Company   67

Maria   89

Telling the Truth   97

Secret Beach   117

Kiss and Tell   127

I Spy   145

23 Hours Back of Beyond   155

Solo   193

A Note on Sources   207

Acknowledgments   211

To Bill—
With gratitude, in love

Author's Note

DEEP among the birch, some miles back from my house in the Adirondack Mountains, is a cabin where a man is said to have lived alone for a quarter century, maybe longer. Then one day, the story goes, he walked out of the woods and disappeared.

I looked for that man in the course of writing this book. I wanted to ask him a few questions. I looked in hospitals and prisons and homeless shelters and a monastery, in one small town and in the wild places around it. I was interested in his experience of solitude, not as an existential dilemma but as a physical fact. And I wanted to know, as he did, about privacy as a quality of life, rather than as a vague, contested, and often rhetorical legal concept, privacy as a matter of rights. The right to privacy is a limited, distinctly American invention. Yet the desire for privacy, anthropologists suggest, appears to be universal. That Americans have codified this desire, elevating it to a right, suggests how vulnerable to each other and to the government we feel, and how strong the desire is to be let alone.

But the language of rights is distorting. It queers our relationship to the thing itself, to privacy, and so to each other, for once we begin to talk about privacy in terms of rights the conversation turns juridical and we want to know how far we can go—how close can we live to our neighbors, how loud can we play our radios, when can't we terminate our pregnancies. The law draws a border between what is permissible and what is not, and pretty soon almost everyone is camped on that line, doing things that are perfectly legal, like sifting through their neighbor's trash, things that decency and propriety would otherwise preclude. But decency and propriety are miles back—too far back to let us see into the window of the woman next door. "It didn't sound like the kind of thing we wanted to be involved in," said an executive in TRW's information services division about the company's perfectly legal decision to sell information to employers about how their employees were spending their money, "but it's what our customers wanted, and all our competitors were doing it."

With few exceptions, the essays in this book avoid discussing privacy in its legal context. Instead, they are meant to turn the conversation away for the moment from the right to be let alone and the protection of that right, to the experience of being left alone, or of not being left alone. It is here that privacy, which in broad terms is the state of being free from the observations, disclosures, and intrusions of others, and solitude, which is the condition of being apart, merge. Privacy, ultimately, is a migration to solitude—to that place where we are fundamentally by ourselves.

These essays are personal. They are not necessarily about me, though some of them are, but all of them are about people's lives—the monks and hermits and prison inmates, the pregnant teenagers, the homeless women, the men with AIDS and their mothers I met when I couldn't find the man who came out of the woods. Together they don't collect into an argument, don't inspire a thesis: privacy, yea or nay; solitude, too much, too little; privacy, threatened, secure. Arguments such as these can be made and have been made, eloquently and compellingly, and on both sides. This is because privacy, which is a good, is not an unqualified good, like, for example, good health. A thoroughly private society would be a cold, disheartening place. Yet privacy, some measure of it, is essential to our souls. It is essential not only to the souls of painters and poets, who thrive in solitude, but to the rest of us, too—individuals whose canvas is our lives.

Wild Ducks,

People, &

Distances

SHORTLY after we were married my husband and I found ourselves outside New York City, driving against traffic, moving to a house on the rim of the wilderness. At the time, the percentage of Americans living in rural areas had never been lower; it's lower now. "Small towns and the countryside are in grave trouble. In an economic sense, a lot of these little places just aren't needed anymore," Calvin Beale, a demographer for the Agriculture Department, told the *New York Times* after the 1990 census revealed that less than a quarter of the population was rural, down from about half at mid-century. We were moving to one of those little places, where the skyline, shingled with granite and pine, and the sky itself, and the woods, deep as night, and night itself are reminders that we are even littler. By dusk, atop the mountain that is its cynosure, you can see that our town is described by two chains of light, and then there is nothing. That nothing is tamarack, birch, and hemlock, swamp maple and swamp and open field; that nothing is the tie that binds.

Recently a Gallup poll asked people, most of whom live in cities and suburbs and are going to stay there, where they would like to live. What they said most was small towns. This is more than a little wistful—they'd probably rather own a Model T, but they're going to buy the Taurus. What happens with that wistfulness, though, is that certain behavior and attitudes common to rural life become, to those who live elsewhere, values. And not only that, they become quaint values, values that one need not then incorporate into one's life because they belong to a different place and time.

I wasn't here then, but when the Crosses' house burned down a few years ago, the people in town got together and built them a new one. The men hammered and sawed; the women made sandwiches and lemonade. When Katie Cross died last winter, I dressed to go to her funeral. It was bitter cold, and when I went to start the car, it wouldn't turn over. I called my nearest neighbor. He drove up a short while later, got out of his car, handed me his keys, and started to walk the mile and a half home.

If "good fences make good neighbors," distance is a kind of fence. It draws people in. A good illustration of this was given to me by a friend when he dropped off his rototiller. ("Are we renting the tiller from him?" I asked my husband. No, he informed me, we were borrowing.) My friend was talking about hitchhiking. "You go out on the highway, ten cars pass you a minute, and you can't get a ride," he said. "Out here maybe two people go by every twenty minutes, but chances are one or the other knows you and picks you up."

Still, there is a way in which we like to be bypassed, to be ignored, which is the allure of cities. The city relieves you of a past. Its promise of anonymity, its indifference to history, offer another kind of space, another kind of distance, one too vast for fencing. Here, no matter how far apart from each other we live, there is a way in which we are always on top of each other. Our general store rents movies. Every so often a mildly risqué film slips in among the Schwarzeneggers and the Stallones—something on the order of *Debbie Does Math*—and nobody rents it. How could they? The preacher might walk in just then, or the plumber, and then there is the man who owns the store, whom they'd have to face to sign it out, and this is not the way they'd like to be remembered. When one of the largest video rental chains in the country announced not long ago that it was inviting the preacher and the plumber over—that is, offering for sale lists of customer names and the movies they borrowed—there was a tremendous outcry from patrons, who had thought no one was looking. The desire to suppress the unedited version of ourselves is as strong, or stronger, than the desire to live it.

It's the unedited version of each other, though, that people seem so often to be after. It's Tom the tailor peeping through the shutter at Lady Godiva riding by

in her glory. It's the tabloids, hiring a fleet of heli-
copters and a man in a llama suit to get a photograph
of the wedding at a Vermont inn of the actors Michael
J. Fox and Tracy Pollan. "Now bad reviews I can
normally handle—you put your work out there and
anybody can take their shot," Fox explained. "But
Tracy and I had never conceived of our wedding as
part of our oeuvre. That's why it hadn't occurred to
us to invite the press." And so the value of the event
increased. We know who you *say* you are, the readers
of the *National Enquirer* must have said to themselves
a few years later, when they handed over eighty-five
cents for the cover story "Michael J. Fox Is a Jerk—
Inside Story of 'Family Ties,' " but since I am not
exactly who I say I am, you must not be who you say
you are either, and I am going to find out the truth.
The quest for these sorts of verities is not limited to
Americans. The British tabloid industry is thriving,
even after *The Sun* had to pay the singer Elton John
$1.7 million for falsely claiming he hired a young male
prostitute, and the editor of *The People* was fired for
publishing photographs of seven-year-old Prince William urinating in a park.

It's not only the thrill of watching the mighty take
a tumble that encourages people to polish their bi-
noculars, though this is part of it. It's also that the
insecurity that comes from realizing there is a difference between the world as it is presented and the world

as it really is has led to the belief that somebody else, somebody who is richer or more famous or sexier, *does* actually know the score, which is why they are richer, more famous, or sexier. It's the belief that these people, or books by them or articles about them, or tracts with titles like "Wealth Without Risk," or dirty movies, or peeking through the shutters, are going to lead to this knowledge. It's the belief that there is just one piece of information remaining between you and your happiness. And so, curiosity becomes a spotlight rather than a lantern, and true mystery melts into the darkness at its edges, and the world is flattened by a single narrow beam.

True mystery is the hooded merganser on the pond behind our house, and what it took for her to get there. True mystery is the kindness of strangers, which is unwonted, and the kindness of neighbors, which is not. In our stretch of woods, you don't have to say much for news to travel, and sometimes you don't have to say anything at all. Once, when my husband was away, I was mailing a letter and the postmaster observed that it was almost time for him to be back from San Francisco. She was right, but I hadn't mentioned he was away, let alone where he was or when he was returning. Another time, the postmaster's assistant told me that she was sometimes accused of reading the postcards that passed through her hands. She said this indignantly, and of course she never would, but I could see why people might have thought it. Somehow, elliptically, we know things about each other.

In the beginning the mysterious intelligence that transformed private information into public knowledge left me feeling vulnerable and unsettled. After all, I came from a place where all natural predators had been extirpated and people looked upon each other with suspicion; where, because there were so many of us, we found safety, not in numbers but in statistics, in being a face in the crowd; where we made certain calculations about walking down this street or that, and talked about the odds of random violence.

Here, where nature still gangs up on people from time to time, where odds makers bet on the vagaries of weather and the power going out, there is no crowd to hide in, and hiding does no good. Cookies arrive on the doorsteps of the sick, and prayers are said, and the postmaster inquires after your absent husband.

New Heaven
and Earth

JANET "Kookie" Driver is hoarse. It is two days after she has led a band of demonstrators across six and a half miles of the Bronx, past the woman wearing a plastic supermarket shopping bag for a skirt, past the men who sleep in abandoned cars, past the ones who are almost too drunk or too high to notice. These are her people. They, like the twenty-five marchers behind her, and like Janet Driver herself, are homeless, or have been homeless, or are on the verge of becoming homeless. . . . "What do we want?"

Janet yells. She is a husky, insistent woman with a brush-cut Afro and Terminator sunglasses.

"Housing," the group answers.

"When do we want it?" Janet asks.   "Now," they respond.

. . .

NOBODY knows how many people are homeless in America. Estimates range from 250,000 to 3 million. The homeless are ubiquitous and elusive. One night during the 1990 census a census taker in Manhattan, along with a reporter and an advocate for the homeless, couldn't find a single homeless person in a city where conservative estimates put the number of homeless men, women, and children at 50,000. The reason for this, said the advocate, Douglas Lasdon, was that on this night, as on any other night, the homeless were indistinguishable from the housed. "There are lots of people just walking down the street or sitting in a diner or movie theater, and you can't tell just by looking if they're homeless or not," he said.

A few years ago New York City's Human Resources Administration came up with a statistical portrait of the city's homeless families: 95 percent are black or Hispanic; 86 percent are headed by women; their average age is twenty-three; 83 percent are supported by public assistance. This portrait bears a marked resemblance to Janet Driver. She is black, receives home relief, and is the mother of four children, three of whom were born when she was a teenager. The resemblance, however, is only partial. She is thirty-eight, single, divorced, and none of her children lives with her. She used to have a job, many jobs—waitress, welder, landscaper, housepainter. She used to own a house. Most recently she has been a resident of a homeless shelter.

The day after the march, Janet goes to a rally at Union Square Park in Manhattan sponsored by an organization called Housing Now!, where she gets an award, and then to an interfaith service honoring homeless leaders at Temple B'nai Jeshurun. During the service the congregation, both homeless and housed, participates in a responsive reading that asks, in part, "Do you believe that decent, affordable housing is a basic human right?" In a single voice the participants answer, "Yes, I do believe."

This belief, that housing is a right, is deeply held by Janet Driver and her friends, and shared by many of those who work on behalf of the homeless. It is a fundamentally American belief, this belief in rights; it is what becomes of a nation with a written, amendable constitution and a philosophical affection for individualism. Yet it will not do. Rights, even natural or God-given ones, often require that governments and legislatures and courts codify them and when they are not codified, they cannot be said to exist. And rights are transient: If they can be given, they can be taken away. To call housing a right is to shift the debate away from the issue at hand—homelessness—to something more abstract—jurisprudence. To call it a right is to misconstrue its real character. Housing is, above all else, a need. It is a need that exists and will continue to exist independent of any right that may satisfy it. But we are uncomfortable with needs unless they are our own. In the language that we share, the language of rights and duties, there is no word for giving people what they need. The words we do have, like *benefits* and *entitlements*, are about granting people what they are owed, and what they are owed is limited—it is a line item in last year's budget. We are lacking the vocabulary to think in broader, more generous terms.

Housing is a need the way glasses are a need for the visually impaired—not necessarily a matter of life or death but something that makes a decent life possible. And it is not a new or modern need. "Even in the crudest neolithic village," writes Lewis Mumford, "the house was always more than a mere shelter for the physical body: It was the meeting place of a household; its hearth was a center of religious ceremony as well as an aid to cooking; it was the home of the household god and the locus of a family's being. . . ." A house is a fixed point, a place to leave from and to come back to.

· · ·

HOME for Janet Driver for the last year has been a tar-shingled and red clapboard three-story building on Webster Avenue in the North Bronx. It is called POTS House, and it is a soup kitchen and shelter for homeless single adults. POTS, which stands for Part of the Solution, is run by a twenty-nine-year-old white man, Tim Boon. Boon has worked with the homeless ever since getting off a bus from Indiana at the age of eighteen, walking from Port Authority to Covenant House, the Times Square shelter for runaway youth, and insisting he be allowed to work there, even though he was the same age as many of the residents, or younger. At Covenant House, Boon met a Catholic priest, Father Ned Murphy, who was making plans to move to the Bronx, not far from Fordham University, to set up a residence for a small number of runaway and throwaway teenage boys. Boon had plans of his own. He wanted to open a soup kitchen—one that did not close, like so many of them, on the weekends.

In 1981 Father Murphy's "family" of young men, including Tim Boon, moved into the first POTS House, on Bedford Park Boulevard. Within a year, Boon and a nun from the Sisters of Charity, Jane Iannuchelli, had opened a seven-day-a-week soup kitchen around the corner on Fordham Road. The soup kitchen and residence cost $40,000 a year to run, and most of the money was raised in church aisles. Four and a half years later, at the height of a real-estate boom in New York that spread even to its fringes, the Fordham Road building was bought by speculators, and POTS House was evicted. The soup kitchen went out of business.

One Sunday morning, three months after the eviction, Father Murphy said mass and preached the sermon at a church in Rye, New York, a wealthy Westchester suburb. He returned to the Bronx that afternoon with the $60,000 Tim Boon needed to buy a rundown storefront on Webster Avenue, where he envisioned setting up a new soup kitchen, a medical clinic, and a temporary residence for both men and women. People from the church in Rye, and students from Fordham, and electricians from the electrical union, and friends of Father Murphy and Tim Boon, and the homeless themselves spent two years taking apart the inside of the building and putting it back together again. The soup kitchen, which serves four hundred meals a day, opened for business in November 1988. The hostel, with six beds for men and six for women, and the medical clinic, opened three months after that. The renovation was adequate enough to bring the building up to code, nothing more. The stairs are steep and rickety, pipes are exposed, the linoleum is rutted, the furniture is mismatched and worn. Yet it is a homely place, not an institutional one—a ramshackle, humming, homely place.

· · ·

THE women's dormitory is long and narrow, like a bowling alley. It has a lounge that faces Webster Avenue, a wide street with a lot of heavy commercial traffic whose noise periodically fills the room. The lounge is furnished with a brown vinyl chair and couch, an ironing board, a color television, and a coffee table with copies of *Reader's Digest* from 1980, one of which has an article entitled "Have Astronauts Found God?" The walls are bare, except for a picture of a pot of gold at the end of a rainbow drawn with Magic Markers on construction paper hung across from the couch, and a schedule of Alcoholics Anonymous and Narcotics Anonymous meetings posted on a bulletin board.

There are two spider plants and a jasmine plant on the windowsill.

The plants belong to Leah Williams, whose bed is at the far end of the floor, the last bed in a line of six in the women's dormitory, which is separated from the lounge by a blue floral-print curtain. Leah has been living at the shelter for more than a year. In that time she has made the space around her bed into her own. The back wall is decorated with certificates of appreciation for her work on behalf of people with AIDS and the homeless. A Teddy bear, a Cookie Monster, a stuffed dog, and other animals crowd her pillow. There are photographs of her twelve-year-old daughter and four-year-old son on the night table. Like some of the other women in the room, Leah has hung her winter coat and jacket from the water pipe that runs the length of the building. They are near enough to the foot of the bed to provide some semblance of privacy in a room without doors. At the other end of the dormitory— which is to say, about twenty-two feet away—Janet's cot, and the space around it, are much the same as Leah's: personal mementoes, clothes crammed into a few shelves, the jerry-built curtain of coats and dresses.

On this night in June, though, the clothes have not deterred Johnny, an eighteen-year-old resident of the men's floor, from sneaking up the back stairs and taking a picture of one of the women as she stepped out of the shower. Or it hasn't stopped him from pretending to take a picture, which is what he claims he was doing to a delegation from the women's floor that has gone downstairs to confront him. The women aren't the only ones who are angry at Johnny. Petey, who has to get up early in the morning for his construction job, is tired of asking him to stop blasting his radio after the nine o'clock cutoff.

"One of us has to die," Petey says. "This morning I wanted to take the guy's head and put it on the train tracks and hold it down until the train comes."

This is not metaphor, not bluster. Petey is a forty-four-year-old Vietnam veteran who, by his own account, spent six months in the psychiatric ward of the VA hospital with post-traumatic stress syndrome; another time he tried to burn down a municipal hospital where he worked as an orderly. This was after he left the VA by the window, on a rope of tightly knotted bed sheets.

Petey, who was born in Puerto Rico, raised in New York, and once lived in Westchester with his wife and four children, has been at POTS for seven months. He says it is heaven compared with where he used to live—a vacant, boarded-up, burned-out tenement in the South Bronx, where he would draw water from a fire hydrant to wash himself of fleas. By day he would pick through the trash, looking for returnable bottles and cans, and when that didn't work out, he would beg.

"I'd blame it on God," Petey says. "I'd go out and beg, and people wouldn't give me something to eat, and I would just cry. At night I would curl up like a caterpillar, say my prayers, and cry and cry. By myself, crying."

When drug dealers and prostitutes started using the building, Petey moved to the D train, which he rode all night, and then to the Bedford Park subway station, not far from POTS House. He began to eat there, then volunteered in the kitchen, and finally moved in.

The one place Petey has not lived in in all his years on the street, the place he refuses to live in, is a public homeless shelter. "A shelter is not fit for a dog because even a dog deserves a home, and I'd love my dog too much to send him there," he says.

. . .

ONE of the shelters where Petey won't live is in a National Guard armory on 168th Street in upper Manhattan, across from the Columbia University medical school and a few blocks from a park where a man was found not long ago living in a cave. Nine hundred men—nine hundred—sleep on army cots in one big room. That's at night. During the day, when only the sick have access to their beds, men sprawl along the corridors of the armory on the concrete floor. Although the room with nine hundred beds is, in its scale, of our age, it is, in most other ways, not unlike Mumford's description of a medieval dwelling: "a general absence of functionally differentiated space . . . [with] scarcely an inkling of two important domestic requirements of the present day: privacy and comfort."

Ten years ago Oscar Newman, an architect with the Institute of Community Design Analysis, testified in court about the conditions he found in another New York City shelter for men, the Keener Building on Ward's Island: "I was surprised to find at eleven o'clock in the morning that the room was in the state it was in," he said. "The beds were not made . . . people were sleeping on the plastic cover of the mattress, and in some instances people were sleeping on the plastic cots without a mattress, and in other instances people were sleeping with the mattress directly on the floor." And, he added, "I found in examining the conditions where you have in excess of eight beds, people stop doing certain activities. They stop cleaning the area around their bed, they stop concerning themselves about litter, they stop concerning themselves about their own grooming. The only activity that they would do was simply to lie on the bed. . . . They just lie there even during the course of the day, not communicating with each other."

It is said that among the Mehinacu of Brazil, where the husband lives with his wife and her family, he shows her parents respect by ignoring them. Perhaps it is the same in homeless shelters. Or perhaps it is as Petey says: "The shelter is death."

. . .

IT is not only homeless men who are put up, for months on end, in school gyms and on military drill floors. Children and their parents are, too. "So I'm all alone there," a man who lost his job after his wife died, leaving him to look after their three small children, told the writer Jonathan Kozol, "in this place with about two hundred cots packed side by side. Men, women, and children, all together. No dividers. There's no curtains and no screens. I have to dress my kids with people watching. When my girls go to the toilet, I can't take them, and they're scared to go alone."

"How would you like to have fourteen people watching you take off your sneakers?" a child in one of the shelters asked a monitor from the New York Citizens' Committee for Children. "Everything we say and do is in front of an audience." In one of these "family shelters" the bathrooms are co-ed; in all of them, stall doors and shower curtains are rare.

. . .

ADVOCATES for the homeless suggest that homeless men, women, and children are crowded together in school gyms to discourage them from seeking public shelter. Even if this is not true, the design of the shelters and the way they are run indicate that the people in charge have figured out that reducing privacy reduces comfort. This equation, between privacy and comfort, holds for those with money as well as those without. What else is a first-class train compartment but more privacy and more comfort? What else is a detached house, a single-bed hospital room, a quiet table in the corner? But for people without money, the equation tends always to have negative outcomes —a bed in a gym, a shower without curtains, no privacy, and nothing comforting.

Though better, it is the same at POTS House, where little goes on out of sight. This was intentional, according to one of the builders. The openness was a means of social control to ensure that residents weren't doing drugs or in other ways breaking the rules. He regrets now that there are only two small partitions in the women's dorm and one in the men's, because he has come to believe that one of the greatest indignities of homelessness is its publicness. People who live in houses, in apartments, in rooms, can retreat at will, and our retreat can be physical—we need not develop some emotional tic to shut out the rest of the world. And in that space we can be alone or we can couple, we can play the harmonica, read trashy books, sneak a chocolate bar. In other words, we can be ourselves.

But this is too abstract. Recently New York City

was sued by a group of homeless people demanding the city provide public toilets. In his affidavit a thirty-eight-year-old resident of a park in the Bronx, a decorated Vietnam veteran named Ramon Gonzales, described one of the humiliations of living out in the open: "Sometimes people see me going to the bathroom and I feel uncomfortable and embarrassed. During the daytime there are usually kids and mothers in the parks, and they think I am flashing them. About two months ago I had diarrhea and was in Central Park. It was a nice sunny day and there were lots of kids with nannies and lots of people around. I couldn't find anywhere to go and was too embarrassed to pull down my pants in front of all the people, so I defecated on myself. I walked around with my pants soiled for about an hour looking for some way to clean myself. Finally I had to take the subway back up to the park in the Bronx where I have some extra clothes stashed. The subway was crowded and the diarrhea was running down my legs. All the people on the train smelled it and moved away from me. I was very embarrassed and felt very bad."

. . .

JANET DRIVER is personally acquainted with the algebra of comfort, dignity, and privacy. Before she got a bed at POTS House she lived in a room of the apartment of a friend of a friend who was addicted to crack and had never gotten around to buying furniture or throwing out the trash, which was knee-deep. Before this she was in jail. That was in Virginia, where she is from.

Although there are no typical homeless people, there are typical stories, and they all seem to begin at the same place. Janet Driver was abused as a child. She was beaten by her stepfather and, at thirteen, raped by him. She was beaten and molested by someone close to her family, who also raped her. At the age of fourteen she had her first child by this man. Her second, two years later. By then she had a problem with alcohol that dated back to the third grade. She dropped out of high school, at seventeen married an alcoholic, had another child before she was eighteen. Her husband beat her. They moved to Detroit. Things got worse. Her drug use accelerated. She went back to school, though, got a high school equivalency diploma, and left her husband. She was twenty-seven. She started free-basing cocaine.

It was cocaine that landed Janet in jail. To get money to buy drugs, she and a friend would go into a store, and one of them would raise a ruckus while the other walked out with a CD player or a cassette recorder, which they would then return for cash. It was one of these outings in 1988, when Janet was thirty-five, that ended in the Hampton City jail. A year later she was

in New York after an all-night bus ride. She had
worked long enough at Wendy's to leave Virginia with
$150 in her pocket, which she figured was enough to
get her established in New York. She hadn't counted
on a week at the Y costing more than that.

So there was the crack den, a month of that, her
first month of sobriety. She started going to Alcoholics
Anonymous at St. Barnabas Hospital, and eating at
the POTS House soup kitchen. At AA they told her
to attend ninety meetings in ninety days and save a
dollar a day, and if she was not satisfied in ninety days,
she'd have ninety dollars with which to get drunk.
Before the three months were up she was living at
POTS, and the money she saved went for a big dinner
she cooked there to introduce the staff of the shelter
to the staff at St. Barnabas. It was then, she says, that
she "started networking."

Janet is sitting in the kitchen where she made that
dinner when she tells this story. It is late at night.
She has just cut into a chocolate bakery cake with white
frosting, pink flowers, and green lettering that says
"Congratulations Kookie!" It is late at night because
she has just returned from her first class at the New
School, an hour away by subway, where she has been
given a scholarship to study. The cake, I assume, is
to congratulate her for that. About two hours later I
find that that's not it at all. It's her anniversary. Today
she has been sober a year.

In the first year of her sobriety, Janet says she has felt like she was on a mission "to get my life together to show my appreciation to everyone who helped me. The corporation is my way of making amends for all the stupid things I did while I was out there." The corporation is the POTS Homesteaders Housing Corporation, an organization she founded to buy abandoned tenements from the city and rehabilitate them with the assistance of the homeless who will eventually live there or in other sweat-equity buildings. Janet is the president. She has been working on a deal for a twelve-room, single-occupancy unit, pressing city officials for months. She understands, though, better than any housing expert or policy analyst, that housing the homeless means more than providing shelter.

"You can't just go from being homeless to living in an apartment—you have to be reeducated, you have to become ready to have a home or you are going to destroy it. You'll still be homeless in your head; it's an attitudinal thing," she says. "And you can't just hand out apartments," she adds. "People won't take care of them. When people struggle to get something, they care about it."

A few years ago a National Institute of Medicine panel issued a report on homelessness that noted that "two recent studies reported a high prevalence of substance abuse (alcohol and other drugs) and major psychiatric disorders among [homeless individual adults in shelters]. Arce et al. examined homeless people in

Philadelphia and diagnosed major mental illness in 40 percent of those studied. When substance abuse, personality disorders, and organic disorders were included among the diagnoses, the figure rose to 78 percent of those studied. Bassuk et al., in a similar study in Boston, reported major mental illnesses (mania, depression, schizophrenia) among 39 percent of those studied; when substance abuse and personality disorders were included among the diagnoses, the figure rose to 90 percent." Thirty-nine percent, 40 percent, 78 percent, 90 percent. These numbers are like speed limits on the autobahn—essentially meaningless except to suggest there is such a phenomenon as limits to speed or that there is widespread drug use and mental illness among the homeless.

More often than not, the solution to homelessness is said to be "three words, housing, housing, housing," to quote Robert Hayes of the National Coalition for the Homeless. This is true, as far as it goes—and given the systematic elimination of affordable low-income housing in the 1980s, it would go far. But not far enough, Janet Driver points out, if people are still homeless in their heads, or if they are as dysfunctional as they were before they became homeless, or as dysfunctional as they became to survive being homeless.

. . .

So Janet Driver is hoarse, two days after she has led a group of twenty-five homeless people and their friends across the Bronx, from one congressman's office to another, demanding political action. We are sitting in the living room of her one-bedroom apartment on Dawson Avenue in the South Bronx. Her apartment. It is three months after we first met at POTS House; she has lived here nine weeks. Her own apartment. Indian summer sneaks around the sheets she has tucked into the windows for curtains and fills the room with a quick light. There is a yellow easy chair in the room and an orange plaid colonial couch with tooled-wood armrests, a Formica desk, and a card table with a bouquet of white carnations on it. There is no indication that this is the home of someone who has spent the better part of the last two years being homeless—but what would that be? There is no evidence that the white dishes weren't all lined up in the blue drying rack in the pink kitchen three months before, that the boards and bricks in the bedroom hadn't yet been combined to make a bookshelf.

Janet's building, 781, sits in a pocket of Dawson Avenue with four other buildings that have been rebuilt and rented to the homeless. It is a pocket on a pair of threadbare pants. The rest of the street looks like the site of a natural disaster, an earthquake, most probably, judging from the fields of rubble and the sinkholes. And the few people out on the street this morning, especially the white girl in the bikini standing under the tracks of the elevated subway, look dazed.

. . .

"THE first time I walked in and shut the door I was overwhelmed," Janet says. "Here was something I had visualized for so long, every night I was in the shelter. I felt very humbled because I knew it didn't have to be me." She shows me the page of her calendar with the date, July 7, 1990. It says, "Moved into 781 Dawson. Thank God!!!"

"At first, when I moved here from the shelter I was a little lonely," she says, "but I'm not lonely anymore. I've learned to turn my loneliness into solitude."

The phone rings. "National steering committee of Housing Now!, speakers' bureau of Interfaith Assemblies, director and founder of POTS Homesteaders. . . . God was with me, what can I say? I want to read some of my poems. When I finish reading these poems, my point will be made," Janet says to the person on the telephone. It is someone from Hunter College, asking her to speak there.

The phone rings again. It is Mircia Apellaniz, the vice president of the POTS Homesteaders, whose bed was next to Janet's in the shelter. She's still a neighbor, three flights up, reunited now with her four children. Leah Williams is in the building, too, but the women haven't seen her since she moved in. She hasn't answered the bell or the notes they slip under her door, hasn't installed a telephone, didn't show up the day she was supposed to get a bed from a social service agency. Her friends think she may be back with her old boyfriend, and back on drugs, and soon may be back on the street.

"One of the rules of the tenants' association, not to let drug dealers into the building, was her idea back at POTS," says Mircia, who has come downstairs. "If you don't comply, you're out. She's annihilating herself."

"Alienating herself," Janet says.

"I meant what I said," Mircia says.

. . .

JANET and Mircia go over to POTS House, where Mircia works as Tim Boon's assistant. They are taking one of the residents, Renee, to an agency in Manhattan where she can arrange to get furniture for her new apartment. She is moving out of POTS House the next day.

It is eleven o'clock, too early for lunch, but the soup kitchen is packed. Maybe fifty people are in there, yet the dining room is quiet in a disorganized way. There are random noises—a person mumbling to himself, another drumming on the table—but no conversations. Jaws are slack, eyes unfocused, faces drawn. It is a wax museum of the down-and-out.

But when Janet Driver enters, it's as if a flash flood were suddenly bearing down on a dry streambed. It's as if the tape were being advanced from "Pause" to "Play." She moves from table to table, touching hands, singing out greetings. She works the room. She wakes them up. These are her people, and she's not going to let them forget it.

"Recovery is not promised to me," I hear her say.

The Place
of the
Solitaries

To get there you drive past the village of Severance and through the town of Paradox, names that make sense when you are going to visit hermits. Then you go five miles one way and nine and a quarter another, look for a stump between two blue spruces, walk half a mile through an open pine forest, turn at the forked birch, cross a stream on a slatted bridge, walk uphill another quarter mile, and listen for her ax or his shovel. Actually, this is not how you get there at all. They asked me not to tell. "Otherwise we wouldn't be hermits, would we?" the one I call Ned says. The other one, Mae, nods in agreement. She is just over five feet, and tough, like beef jerky. She wears blue jeans and a striped man-tailored shirt. Her hair is clipped short and shaped like a helmet. It is white. She is sixty-eight. She has been a hermit for forty years.

The same with Ned. He has merry blue eyes and a gap-toothed grin, and he's tall and as thin as a split rail. He is so thin, in fact, that his green cotton pants, which are held up by suspenders, look like waders. He's got on a plaid flannel shirt and work boots. He is seventy years old. He wears his clothes sincerely.

". . . [W]e readily attribute some extra virtue to

those persons who voluntarily embrace solitude, who live alone in the country or in the woods or in the mountains and find life sweet," the aspiring recluse John Burroughs wrote in a volume called *Indoor Studies*. "We know they cannot live without converse, without society of some sort, and we credit them with the power of invoking it from themselves, or else of finding more companionship with dumb things than ordinary mortals." But with Ned and Mae it is not this way, for they have each other. They are solitaries together, but solitaries nonetheless. They live deep in the forest in a house of their own construction. They are self-sufficient. They would prefer not to know you.

. . .

NED and Mae were not born to this life. They had conventional upbringings—as conventional as upbringings were during the Depression. After high school in Herkimer, New York, where they were sweethearts, Mae worked as a clerk in a five-and-ten-cent store and Ned strung lines for the telephone company. His health was bad, he had kidney disease, and a doctor suggested that a month or two in the woods would be restorative. If two months might help, the newlyweds reasoned, what about two years, or twenty-two? They quit their jobs and moved to the south-western end of the Adirondack Park, where Ned's father, a lawyer, had been given a parcel of lakefront in exchange for legal work. There was a summer camp on the lake, and the two of them found work there as carpenters and caretakers. They started an egg and chicken route. Ned tied flies and sold them through the mail. But after a while the lake got "too busy," Ned says, and they decided to move.

"We took out a map of the Adirondacks and circled the places that interested us," he recalls. In their spare time they visited each one, camping out or sleeping in their car in order to see it through varied grades of light. It took three years before they found the land they wanted. "B'gosh, we liked it over here," Ned says. They sold their house on the water and bought 175 acres of ridge and hill.

"He shouldn't be here," Mae says of Ned. "The doctor told his father he wouldn't see forty. That was fifty years ago. See what the Adirondack woods can do for you."

But it's not just Ned. The Adirondack woods have long been hospitable to hermits. In *Tales of Hamilton County*, local historians Ted Aber and Stella King devote page after page to the likes of Noah John Rondeau, Ezra Bowen, Laramie Harney, and Adirondack French Louie—men who lived in the interior by their wits and the good graces of the land, eighteenth-century men born a century too late, men who would have been a century late no matter when they were born. Once, according to Aber and King, a consumptive city dweller came to spend the winter in French Louie's cabin in the hope of regaining his strength. As soon as he arrived he tacked a calendar to the wall near his bed. "It was the first thing that met the hermit's eyes when he reached the door. Instantly he snatched the offensive decoration from the wall and shoved it into the stove. 'If you stay with me, tomorrow will be just like today, and today just like yesterday—no different,' he pronounced."

It is time, as much as distance, that distinguishes the hermit's life. It is Thoreau sitting in his doorway from sunrise till noon. It is Rousseau, self-exiled on the island of Saint-Pierre, trading philosophy for flowers. ("Botany is the ideal study for the idle, unoccupied solitary," he writes; "a blade and a magnifying glass are all the equipment he needs for his observations. . . . This ideal occupation has a charm which can only be felt when the passions are entirely at rest. . . .") It is Ned and Mae spending two years laying nine hundred feet of pipe by hand from a stream to their house. It is Ned and Mae spending an entire winter peeling the bark of the balsams, oaks, maples, and pines they felled in the warm seasons before. They brought these logs down without benefit of a chain saw or a skidder or horses. And they raised them up again to build their house without using a crane. Six years—that's how long it took them.

It is a playful corduroy house on a rise, with windows that open to every point of the compass, to tree and bird and sky and hill. Inside there is a root cellar, and a mud room, a bathroom, a bunk room, a kitchen and hearth on the first floor, and a bedroom, study, and sitting room on the second. The house has running water—hence the nine-hundred-foot pipe— some of which is left to bake in a holding tank off the kitchen, and an indoor toilet, a concession, they say, to their advancing ages, though Mae still prefers the outhouse. They built this hermitage when they were in their sixties.

Before this they lived in a similar two-story home-made dwelling, but without plumbing. It is downwind from this one, overlooking a pond. They built the pond, too, clearing the half acre with picks and shovels, digging down six feet, prising the stones with their hands, using the stones to make a dam and a retaining wall and a walkway. They have built other things as well: a log garage, a summer kitchen, three garden plots, two wood-fired hothouses, a storage shed, a carpentry workshop, a composter, and three pavilions filled with enough split wood to keep them going for a year if need be.

Ned and Mae are off the power grid. They don't have electric lights, telephones, a toaster, or a washing machine. If they did, they wouldn't have anything to plug them into. "I guess most people would go crazy," Mae says. For them it is the other way around. The absence of electricity doesn't simplify things; it keeps them simple. Day begins at sunrise and ends with darkness. What do they do then? "We make popcorn every night in the winter," Ned says. "Well, that takes a lot of the evening. I guess it's what you'd call kind of a slow lifestyle."

When Emerson writes in "Self-Reliance," "The civilized man has built a coach but has lost the use of his feet," he suggests that people like Ned and Mae, who are fleet, are uncivilized, and this is true. Before everything else, civilized man (and woman) is a consumer. He lives in a market economy, he feels bound to do his part. Not Ned and Mae. They have taken a lien on nature's capital. They have a three-season refrigerator a few yards from their door—a galvanized tub sunk in a swift, cold stream—and a winter refrigerator indoors, which captures the frigid air of outdoors. They can't afford a "real" refrigerator; their income is three or four thousand dollars a year, about half the amount the state welfare office pays to individuals on home relief. In conventional, civilized terms they are dirt-poor. But poverty is a matter of desires as well as of means. Ned and Mae *would be* poor if they wanted a 16-cubic-foot white enamel frost-free refrigerator or a ten-cycle washing machine. What they want instead is to spend the afternoon in the sun, kneading their dirty clothes in a metal basin. What they want is to have as few clothes to wash as possible. And so they are not poor. Wood that you chop for fuel is said to warm you twice, first in the splitting, then in the burning. In the same way, Ned and Mae say that they are enriched by their wants.

. . .

A FEW years ago, on December 25, a neighbor hiked in on snowshoes to wish the hermits Merry Christmas and was treated to a sermon denouncing the holiday. Every day is a celebration, they grumbled. No day is a holiday if you have to work so hard at it, and so on. Chastened, the neighbor retreated. A few days later, walking in the woods, Ned and Mae found a small package, a gift, hanging from a tree. "I guess she was too scared to hand it to us," Ned says, laughing.

He can laugh. He takes himself seriously, but not grimly. He doesn't confuse their way of life with a religion and make it an orthodoxy or a mission. (He doesn't tell you their way is the true way because he probably doesn't think you are up to many of its truths.) Nor does he confuse religion with God. Religion is the creation of people—to Ned it is as artificial as electric light. God is the creator of the world he holds dear and *is* the light. In the poems Ned writes, this theme plays like a fugue. "High up in the mountains a fir tree stands / By a lakelet beneath a bright star— / The icy wind shivers its snow-laden hands, / Sparkling and glittering in light from afar. . . . /

41

Other fir trees glory in tinsel and gold / For 'tis Christmastime all over the land, / But none are more loved in heaven above / Than this wildling cared for by God's own hand." The title of the poem is "God's Christmas Tree."

Most of Ned's poems and essays exalting the natural world and lamenting its destruction, as well as his gardening tips, and Mae's too, can be found in a little index-card-sized magazine they put out on a hand-cranked mimeograph machine in the sixties and seventies called *Backwoods Journal.* ("We thought other people might be interested in doing what we were doing," Ned says. Or at least daydreaming about it.) It cost two dollars a year for six issues, and at its peak there were a few hundred readers across the country whose letters found their way to the hermits' post-office box to request a subscription. A typical issue had thirty-five articles spread over sixty pages, most of which were written by Ned and Mae, using six or seven pseudonyms. (Their real names never appeared in the publication.) Rhubarb, the dangers of lead shot, winter camping, and migrating geese were popular subjects. There were no ads, but there was a Personals column. (From a man in Greeley, Pennsylvania: "I'm looking for a Birthday Twin to correspond with and compare notes on our trail through life, a person who was born October 10, 1911, the same day as I. I was an only child as my Mother passed on shortly after my birth. I'm married to a wonderful wife.") Ned did all the artwork in the magazine—pen-and-ink portraits of pine martens and coyotes, sketches of waterfalls and mountains—and though he was not trained as an artist, it is clear that he has a gift for this, too. In another life he might have been able to parlay it into a career and consider himself blessed to be able to work at what he loved.

. . .

AFTER they turned over *Backwoods Journal* to a couple of homesteaders who had been regular contributors, and the homesteaders found it harder to put out a magazine than to live in a tent in the mountains in winter and gave it up, Ned and Mae began to sing. Putting their poems to music, they recorded "Songs of the Wildwood" on a battery-operated, dual-head boom box, from which they then made a bunch of copies, one at a time. The album is dedicated to ". . . those folks everywhere who find inspiration in unspoiled wild lands." On it, Ned sings melody in a wobbly baritone and Mae joins in with a thin soprano, and the overall effect, which is to make you want to turn off the tape player and go for a strenuous hike, is probably what they wanted to accomplish anyway.

But why shouldn't they sing, and even sing badly, especially when they have something to say? ("When life becomes a weary thing, and each new day is hard to bear, take your burdens to the hills, and you will find them lighter there . . ." begins one song.) And why shouldn't they write poems? It is symptomatic of how civilized we have become that poetry must now be written by poets. But if poetry is left to the poets, it means that something else, picking apples, say, is left to the apple pickers, and not only don't we get good poems about harvesting apples, we get a society that believes that apple pickers can't write poetry— which is what we have. But not Ned and Mae. They have the society of each other, and they have poems, and they have fresh apples, and no one to tell them they can't.

. . .

WHEN Thoreau went to Walden Pond to live for two years, it was a young man's experiment. When the time was up, he quit his cabin and moved back to Concord and got on with his life. Ned and Mae were about thirty when they settled on their land, and it was no more an experiment than tilling the soil is an experiment for a farmer. It's like the difference between dating and marriage, Thoreau's retreat and Ned and Mae's. The hermits are wedded to their life in the woods. It's a marriage that's not about what they don't have (central heat, newspapers, ice cream) but what they do (buffleheads on their pond, a pond), and it's not about what they have given up (children, light bulbs), but how to use what they have to make what they need.

Ned shows off his tomato plants, which are still bearing fruit in the late fall, and his cucumbers and lettuce. He mentions the filtration system he rigged up to collect leaves from the pond and points out a ground-floor skylight he built to illuminate trips to the root cellar. He seems genuinely surprised that the things he knows are not common knowledge. Maybe five or six people visit a year, mostly family. "My sister comes and wants to go shopping," Mae says. It's as if she had heard of the practice but can't quite picture it. They don't get out of the woods much. When they do, encounters with their own kind send them back to seek the fellowship of the wind and the whippoorwill. They are happy there. Not gleeful, get-out-the-noisemakers happy, but happy as larks, or buntings.

"We felt kind of funny at first, living this way," Mae says, "but not anymore." Forty years in the woods earning a life, not a living. "A lot of people, I think, wished they would have done it."

A Room of
One's Own

THE day my letter reached him, Robert Stark had been an inmate of the Louisiana State Penitentiary at Angola for seven years, seven months, and nine days. He had been sentenced to die in the electric chair, but after numerous appeals his sentence had been reduced to life imprisonment. When he was nineteen, Robert Stark killed a man during a liquor store holdup—shot him between the eyes, the pathologist's report says. Whether he intended to kill the man or not was the question put to the second jury who heard the case. Their indecision compelled the judge to sentence Stark to life in prison without the possibility of parole, probation, or suspension of sentence, instead of to death by electrocution. Robert Stark will die in prison anyhow, though no time soon. He is thirty-four years old.

Stark's spiritual adviser, a nun who works with death row inmates, put me in touch with him. I wrote him a letter full of questions, but really, I wanted to know one thing: What is it like to live in a cell in one of the most notorious prisons in the country? I assumed he would be eager to tell me. This may have been naive, but it was not immediately, apparently naive.

More than a few times in the two months it took before he wrote back, I wondered what—not how—he was doing. I wasn't thinking about what, specifically, he was doing either. I was thinking that whatever it was, it couldn't be taking all of his time. I was thinking that if there was one thing Robert Stark had in droves, it was time.

. . .

IN 1989 a thirty-two-year-old French woman, a researcher of sorts, crawled into a cave in the South of France in an attempt to live in isolation for 111 days. She was wired from head to toe with electrodes as well as with a rectal probe, required to produce gallons of urine for testing and to go through certain mental and visual routines daily. The point was to remove her from time as it is commonly measured and see what happened. What happened was that within days, day ceased to exist. She would be up for forty hours and sleep for thirty-four and call it one day. She had no idea. "I feel myself slipping into a somber lethargy, a dull numbness," she wrote after waking from one of these extended naps. "The true problem is loneliness. Naturally it's loneliness. Also you think about your life. You may think to your past, to your future, what you want to do. You have time to think, you know? You're a thinking machine when you are alone."

In his first letter to me Robert Stark wrote the same

thing in a different language. "I spend most [days] sleeping with the past—thinking of things that might have been. Moreover, from time to time I lie . . . questioning my very existence." I have never met Robert Stark or seen his photograph, but in my mind I picture him as a bear, huddled in his cave, waiting out an endless winter. This conceit is my own. It is easier, sometimes, to think of a man as an animal than as a man; because we're sentimental about animals it is easier to forgive their trespasses.

In that first letter Stark explained why he hadn't written sooner: "Your letter was received a few days before I found myself in a rather bloody physical confrontation with another inmate. My opponent received 'eight' or 'nine' puncture wounds. However, he'll live. What sparked this, you're wondering? Well, I'd like to be more explicit, but to make a rather long story 'short,' let's just say that this individual . . . knew not his limitations. . . . Been doing isolation time since the twenty-third of March."

How is one to receive such information? A man tells you he has pushed something sharp into the flesh of another man eight or nine times—pushed it in and pulled it out and *pushed it in again*. He tells you this to explain why he hasn't been able to write, the way he might tell you he's been laid up with the flu. Your first reaction—horror—is quickly replaced by something like courtesy. You realize you are in a country whose customs are foreign to you, and you don't want to offend.

Sometime later Stark sent picture postcards of the place where he lives. They were not standard, glossy, wish-you-were-here kinds of cards; they were pieces of pink paper topped with the heading

LOUISIANA
DEPARTMENT OF PUBLIC SAFETY AND CORRECTIONS/
LOUISIANA STATE PENITENTIARY
DISCIPLINARY REPORT.

Each gave an aerial view of the topography—the same view. This confused me at first—it was as if a visitor had gone to New York City and taken pictures only of the traffic at Times Square. Then I realized that this was the point: From this one perspective you could make out the entire lay of the land.

7-28-90 "On the above date and time the above name and number inmate was given several direct Orders (sic) to take his belongings off the shelf in his cell by Sgt. Randall Dubonette. On the next Routing Round that I made the Inmate still had his belongings on the shelf. I then wrote the Inmate up. Rule violated: aggravated disobedience."

7-20-89 "On the above date and approximate time while I, Sgt. Tedesco, was shaking down inmate Stark's cell I found 1 cigarette lighter and six (6) white pills. These pills had Barr on one side and the numbers 419 on the other side. Said pills were identified to be those which inmate Stark takes one (1) three (3) times a day, therefore this inmate had two (2) days' supply in his cell. All these items were confiscated by security. Rule violated: contraband."

None of the guards have handwriting half as neat as Robert Stark's. His penmanship is controlled and deliberate, as if each letter were a breath, as if each breath mattered. He writes that the bars of the isolation cells are dark green, that the bed is bolted to the wall, three feet from the floor, that the ceiling is "dingy white, from years of neglect," and there are no windows. Isolation is like having "hell all to yourself," he says. He has to wear a white jumpsuit; undershorts and socks are forbidden. Magazines and newspapers are forbidden. Combs are forbidden. Ballpoint pens are forbidden. Talking is sometimes allowed, depending on the attitude of the guards, but he can never see whom he is talking to. He is led to and from the shower in leg irons and handcuffs. He describes this sparely, without an extra adjective, as if to say, it's bad enough as it is.

Stark's description chastens me. "What is the best thing about solitary confinement?" I asked in an early letter. "I can't think of anything," he said flatly. It occurs to me that I have been thinking of isolation as Yaddo without cloth napkins, as a kind of retreat. "I am the convict-writer," Lou Torok declares in his autobiography, *Straight Talk from Prison*, and indeed, there is a picture of the author at his typewriter in his cinder-block cell. It's easy to be misled by this. Enough books have been written in prison to make it seem congenial to a certain sort of literary work, and it is —to writing books about prison. Even that great convict-writer, the Reverend Dietrich Bonhoeffer, held by the Nazis in solitary confinement at Tegel Prison, ceased working on his *Ethics*, and turned instead to composing prayers and sermons for his fellow prisoners. "You want to know more about my life here," he wrote to his parents in May 1943, two years before his execution. "To picture to oneself a cell does not need much imagination—the less you use, the nearer the mark you will be."

It's hard to remember, or to believe, that solitary confinement was once a prison *reform*, that in the eighteenth century it was favored by groups like the Philadelphia Society for Alleviating the Miseries of Public Prisons, and men like the architect of the Richmond jail, Thomas Jefferson. Adapting European models of incarceration, they sought to build penitentiaries instead of prisons, places where each inmate, alone with himself and his Bible, would be forced to confront his misdeeds as well as his maker. " 'Do you find it difficult to endure solitude?' " Alexis de Tocqueville and Gustave de Beaumont asked a prisoner in solitary in the course of their research for *On the Penitentiary System in the United States and Its Application in France.* " 'Ah, sir, it is the most horrid punishment that can be imagined!' " " 'Of what do you think most?' " " 'Of religion; religious ideas are my greatest consolation.' " The system might have been said to be working, but the Frenchmen were not entirely convinced. "Solitude applied to the criminal, in order to conduct him to reformation by reflection, rests upon a philosophical and true conception. But the authors of this theory had not yet founded its application upon those means which alone could render it practical and salutary," they wrote. Solitary confinement, they concluded, "corrupted by indolence." While this may not seem an especially loud blast, it was issued just four years after the first stone was laid at the Philadelphia Penitentiary in Cherry Hill—a $750,000, four-hundred-cell monument to the glories of penance. It took another foreign journalist with an interest in American prisons, the Englishwoman Jessica Mitford, looking at the eighteenth-century reforms with more than a century of dispassion, to sound taps: "Unfortunately for the good intentions of the Quakers, things began to go wrong from the very beginning. So many convicts went mad or died as a consequence of the solitary regime that by the mid-nineteenth century it was generally abandoned. . . ." But not at the Louisiana State Penitentiary, not for men like Robert Stark.

I write Stark another letter, and then another, and

for every two I send out, I get one back. After a while I decide this is not the most productive way to conduct an interview, so I write to the warden asking if I can talk with Stark in person. Apparently the warden is a very busy man because he writes back immediately. He says no. Which is how I end up closer to home, in Art Leonardo's office at the Great Meadow Correctional Facility in Comstock, New York, looking at photographs of men in striped prison pajamas at a construction site. The site is Great Meadow. These are the men who built the maximum-security prison eighty years ago.

The building they put up sits on about a hundred acres of rich, alluvial farmland, five miles from the border with Vermont and five hours from New York City, where most of the present inmates are from. It is a massive structure that from a distance appears to be made of Cotswold stone. Up close its yellow bricks look like dentures stained by tobacco. Inside it is dank and dim and feels as though it were underwater. Or maybe it is just that when you walk through the door you begin to worry that you will drown.

Although Comstock is no showpiece—inmates complain of rats and roaches and each other ("I saw a guy killed here because he was wearing the wrong-colored sweatshirt," one of them told me; "I saw a guy killed for a towel," someone else said)—Mr. Leonardo, the superintendent, has arranged for me to take a tour of the facility and to talk to a few of the 1,544 inmates about what it's like to live there.

A female social worker walks me through the tiers. Inmates angle mirrors to see who is coming. They watch us as we pass. We are on parade here. My skin chafes as if it were too tight, too revealing. To distract myself, I count the number of paces it takes to walk from one side of a cell to the other. Two. It would take three steps, I figure, to walk from the front of each metal cage to the toilet at its rear.

Mr. Leonardo explains that in other states two or three men are confined to a room this big. How *big* is that? As big as a king-sized mattress. "The cell is their home, their house, their crib," he says. He explains that the cells may seem small to us, but that for many of the prisoners this is the first time they've had a place of their own. He is a reasonable man, with an open, jocular manner, and he genuinely believes this. "You've got a sense of security in a cell. In a dorm setting you don't know if someone is going to assault you or cuddle up to you. If they ever get me," he says, "I want to be put in a cell, not in a dormitory."

The dormitory the warden is thinking of is just down the road from Great Meadow at the Washington Correctional Facility, a medium-security prison. If you ignore the belt of razor wire at its margins, Washington looks like the branch campus of a state university. The grounds are clean, the lawns well tended. Inmates—

mostly young, mostly black, wearing green chinos and hooded sweatshirts and hi-top sneakers—stroll from one low-slung brick building to the other along flowered paths.

The dormitories at Washington are airy, unpartitioned rooms built for fifty men but housing ninety, who sleep in bunk beds stacked like checkers. The dormitories are pleasant enough, and awful enough, to bring Sartre's play, *No Exit*, to mind. ("There's no need for red-hot pokers. Hell is—other people.") No one is ever free from scrutiny or from the sound of ninety men breathing. "Sometimes I will stay awake until three in the morning, when everyone else is asleep, and pretend I am alone," one inmate told me. The first thing he is going to do when he gets released, he says, is go into a room with a door and shut it.

. . .

"I AIN'T never going back to a dorm," Wayne says. He has been at Great Meadow for seventy days in a punishment block where inmates are confined to their cells twenty-three hours a day. The other hour they are allowed to exercise in dog runs. Seventy-one days ago, before the guards found a weapon among his belongings, he was one of the young men jogging from the field house to the library to the mess hall at Washington.

"In a cell you've got more privacy," Wayne says.

"You've got more chance to look into your own self because you're there by yourself. You get something to read, you can elaborate on that, or if you're not much of a reader, you can look back over the course of your life and think back to the reason you're in here."

The reason Wayne is in here, aside from the shank in his locker, has to do with money. He says he stole one million five hundred thousand dollars in thirty-two heists. Maybe he did. Maybe he'd like to believe he did. He's a small, jumpy man in his mid-thirties whose eyes dart this way and that, like fish in a tank. He'll be eligible for parole in a year. Until then, he says, he's going to lie in his cell and "picture me out on the ocean like Robinson Crusoe. My girl went to get a steak, but she got lost so I might as well read till she gets back."

YEARS before I wrote to Robert Stark or visited Comstock and Washington, I was interested in the architecture of prisons, in the alchemy of steel and concrete, in forced work, forced solitude, punishment and reform. I was interested in the architecture of prisons because, at the time, everyone I was meeting had done time. That was my job, to help people who had just been released from jail find work and, you know, become productive members of society. We would pay them a little more than welfare to gut abandoned buildings and paint hopscotch boxes on playground asphalt. We would provide something called "supportive services." Or, rather, my office mate, Claude, an ex-offender himself, would. Claude was a lean man, a sharp dresser, with a goatee and an ample head of hair and a special charm with women. He would pull up his pants leg and pull down his sock. He would take your hand and run it along his calf. You would notice it felt like a dirt road after a heavy rain, like brambles, like a Thomas's English muffin, like a corroded exhaust pipe. Still holding your hand, he would tell you: "This is where the bartender left his signature, in bone chip and lead shot. This is where the police left theirs. Would you like to feel my thigh?"

The project we were working on was a failure. The government knew this and continued to send money. The parole office knew it and continued to send men fresh from Rikers Island and Comstock and Attica. It was a failure because a large portion of these ex-offenders became offenders again, landing back in jail in numbers comparable to those who had not had the benefit of our program. No one seemed to care. Aggregate statistics were abandoned, and the emphasis shifted to individual successes, and to the good our work crews were doing for the community. Which is why I perked up when Gary Filion, the superintendent of the Moriah Shock Incarceration Facility in Mineville, New York, told me that although minimum-security prisons like his do not reduce the rate of recidivism, they do not do so in a cost-effective manner. He said that shock incarceration saves the state something like $10 million a year, and that while it is impossible to know for sure, it might be saving lives, too.

In the Bible Moriah is the place God sent Abraham to sacrifice Isaac, his son. In New York Moriah is where judges send first- and second-time nonviolent felons under thirty. Sacrifice is part of the ritual. Moriah is a prison run like boot camp. It's six months of sir this and sir that, an hour of push-ups in the parking lot before dawn, eight minutes to eat and anything not eaten poured down the front shirt pocket, six hours of clearing brush and painting churches, four hours of group therapy, bed inspection, drug inspection, locker inspection, a rule for walking through the cafeteria line (side step), a rule for smoking (at attention), a rule for eye contact between inmates and staff (punishable). Six months. That is the bait judges hold out to these young men: six unremitting months here, or a year or two or three hanging out at a place like Washington. Then he tugs the line. He explains that they can quit at any time, but if they do, they'll have to serve out their full sentences somewhere else.

OFFICER (*standing two inches from inmate's nose, shouting*): What are you in for?

INMATE (*expressionless, staring straight ahead*): Sir, for selling crack, sir.

OFFICER: How much were you making a day?

INMATE: Sir, two thousand dollars a day, sir.

OFFICER: Are you going to make it [*through Moriah*]?

INMATE: Sir, yes sir.

OFFICER: What are you going to do when you get out?

INMATE: Sir, get a nine-to-five, sir.

OFFICER: A nine-to-five what, knucklehead?

INMATE: Sir, a nine-to-five job, sir.

. . .

"WE don't use the word *rehabilitation* anymore," says Capt. George Thorne. "The new word is—now, let's see, what's the new word?—oh, yes, the new word is *abilitation*."

Captain Thorne has been a corrections officer for thirteen years. He is the top officer at Moriah, second in command only to the superintendent, and he is the only black man on the staff. "I'm a role model for these young men," Captain Thorne says. "I tell them there are people who don't want you to succeed, and if you give up they win and you lose." Captain Thorne tells them to be wary of two-hundred-dollar sneakers and designer clothes. "I tell them, your wife doesn't care about getting the car, the house, the fur. What she really cares about is having you there. I tell them, buy the suit at K Mart."

It is Captain Thorne who points out the pile of rocks

at the bottom of an expansive, grassy slope. The rocks are as big as full moons. "We call them learning experience rocks," he says. "If you forget your ID you have to tape it to a rock and carry the rock around all day. You do that today, you're not going to forget your ID tomorrow." The captain also points out a six-foot log at the entrance to one of the dormitories and explains that when two inmates argue they are "put on the log" and have to spend the day lugging around the log together.

It is an unlikely prospect, that if you remove city punks to a rugged woodland for six months, knock the wind out of them, and lock them in a hammer hold, they will learn to work together, that they will gain self-respect. Can it be as simple as institutional tough love? Apparently not. As Superintendent Filion admits, inmates of shock camps return to prison at the same rates as inmates of other kinds of facilities. But maybe that is beside the point. Once they get through this program, it is theirs for keeps. It stays with them, the way the wounded have the war.

．．．

"MA'AM, I'm going home tomorrow, ma'am."

"Ma'am, I was an accomplice to a robbery, ma'am."

"Ma'am, yes, drugs, ma'am."

"Ma'am, in the beginning the whole platoon resisted, ma'am."

"Ma'am, we started with forty-eight. We're down to thirty-five men, ma'am."

"Ma'am, I learned faith here. I feel this is a God-given program, ma'am."

"Ma'am, some of the drill instructors are actually proud of us, ma'am."

"Ma'am, my whole family is driving up from Brooklyn for graduation tomorrow, ma'am."

"Ma'am, it's a seven-hour drive, ma'am."

. . .

THE day after this conversation, the graduating platoon rises at 5:30, stands at attention in their underwear, makes their beds, brushes their teeth and dresses in under eight minutes, reports to the parking lot for an hour of push-ups and jumping jacks, side-steps through the breakfast line. The ones who look directly at a kitchen worker or corrections officer in the mess hall eat standing up facing a wall on which two eyes the size of beach balls have been painted. After breakfast they trade their green prison-issue uniforms and black work boots for what they call their Century 21 suits—tan blazers and brown slacks and black dress shoes. They pack.

Parents, wives, girl friends, and children sit in the gym on plastic prison-made chairs. Maybe it is the first graduation ceremony they have ever attended, so they don't notice the absence of diplomas. Superintendent Filion addresses the inmates. "You've made it through this challenge," he tells them, "but the real challenge is going to begin tomorrow." He explains why they have done things at Moriah the way they have. He tells them what they need to make it "out there." It is not a job or a place to live—it is love. He speaks for fifteen minutes. Then they are free.

THE woman who went into the cave killed herself. A year after completing the experiment, in January 1990, she took some pills, lay down in the front seat of her van, which was parked on a Parisian street, and went to sleep for good. "It was a risk that came with this experiment—to become half crazy, to become schizophrenic," she had told a radio interviewer two days before. "It didn't happen to me. But maybe it's a time bomb—I won't say anything more about it."

About ten months after that, I received Robert Stark's last letter. He had recently come out of "the dungeon" again, he said, only to find that while he was gone, someone had taken some of his belongings, including my letters. He also said that "things have begun to come together for me, or so it seems." I sent him a check for fifteen dollars along with Christmas greetings.

In Solitude,
for Company

VIGILS. At this hour, when it shouldn't be, the darkness is divisible. It parts over the choir monks standing in their stalls singing: "Lift up your hands to the holy place and bless the Lord through the night." It opens, like a yawn, in the balcony, above the retreatants following along in their psalm books. It is quarter past three. The bells issue their report. The sound is a penance for those who are not monks or farmers. So is the light, broadcast from lamps along the church walls. We who are not monks sing, "Some lay in darkness and in gloom, prisoners in misery and chains." We who are not farmers sing, "He led them forth from darkness and gloom, and He broke their chains to pieces." The sanctuary fills with solemn words chanted on three notes; we are like towhees and cardinals, relying on the same three tones sung in the same order to carry what we say. The sound rises on these drafts and hangs beneath the rafters. It is the only adornment in the church, which is a deep rectangular well made of whitewashed brick. A picture of Mary rests on an easel, halfway to the tabernacle. There there is a freestanding gold cross, three feet high. This could be Ely Cathedral after the Protestant reformers were through with it, so few are the icons. But it is a Roman Catholic church, the church of the Abbey of Our Lady of Gethsemani, a Trappist monastery fifty miles south of Louisville, Kentucky. Gethsemani is the home of seventy-seven monks, most of whom stand in the choir, singing, "Yours is the day and Yours is the night. It was You who appointed the light and the sun." Robed in white with black scapulars, they stand in four rows, two on the right, two on the left. Left and right face each other, like the palms of hands knit in prayer. "It was You who fixed the bounds of the earth, You who made both summer and winter," they sing. The words are indistinct. They are recombinant; together they make some other language, with round vowels and soft consonants, that needs no translation.

It is something like this: One of the monks, who is not in the choir and never attends church, was sent to Brazil for six weeks on monastery business, and while he was there, he found himself drawn to mass and lauds and vespers every day, although he knew no Portuguese. Call it transcendent or call it spectral or call it holy; it is the same. You don't have to be Catholic or Christian or even particularly religious to understand it. You don't have to understand it. You recognize, early on, that your understanding is not what is needed. This is their petition, their prayer. Make of it what you will, they seem to be saying.

Up in the balcony we are one beat behind. It is a

sign of our distance; we are new to this, no matter who we are and where we came from or why—we thirty-two women on retreat. For the monks it is routine. Vigils is the first of the seven offices they sing each day. It is called the nightwatch, which is literal, for after it begins there is no more sleeping.

They bow at the waist. They sing, "The God that was, that is, and is to come, at the end of the ages." Their heads are tonsured. Some have beards, but even so, it is difficult to distinguish one from the other. It is not that they are faceless, it is that they wear one face. It is not an especially angelic or saintly face, as you might expect. It is mortal, almost frail.

LAUDS. Reassembled, we sing, "O God, arise above the heavens; may Your glory shine on earth!" The sun has not yet risen, though the dark has yielded some. Early morning is the best time to pray, the prior, Father Felix, has told me. Prayer is his vocation; it is what he *does*. The early hours are best because the quiet is enfolded. Later in the day the lamb of silence must lie next to the roar of the rest of the world. It must hear, for instance, the sigh of air brakes as the eighteen-wheelers drive past the sign that says "Gethsemani . . . 1848 . . . Noted for Silence, Labor, Prayer," and are waved through the gate to deliver supplies for the mail-order cheese and fruitcake business that supports the monastery. It must hear, from the bakery, the clatter of pans, the hosannas to the Cincinnati Reds. In general, though, the monks do not talk, nor do they want to, and neither do you when you are there. When you hear your own voice, it is trolling lines like "He hurls down hailstones like crumbs. The waters are frozen at His touch; He sends forth His word and it melts them: at the breath of His mouth the waters flow." Otherwise it is still. You become proprietary about this stillness. You find that you don't want conversation. You find that you are pleased that all the chairs in the dining room face the same direction—away—and that, even so, the table out of sight behind the beam is the one most sought, often by you. When you hear voices in the garden below your bedroom window you don't move toward them as if you were parched and they were water; you shut the window despite the heat. You realize it is easier to think kindly about strangers if you need not talk to them or hear them; you realize that silence is a great equalizer, eliminating disagreements about politics and inferences made from accents. You worry, aloud, if there isn't something misanthropic to this. "The ideal is if we can learn to be friendly with an economy of means. Here we can live in a community and have solitude, thanks to the silence," Father Felix says in his gentle, deliberate voice, and you find yourself nodding, nodding, nothing more.

He also says that silence is the road to take if you're

looking to pray. What he doesn't say is that you get there anyway, without looking. First you hear yourself singing, "The ends of the earth stand in awe at the sight of Your wonders. The lands of sunrise and sunset You fill with Your joy." You are clear on this—it is singing, not praying. In a few hours you are walking through a fallow field. In the distance you see a hogback mountain ridge, bristling with tall, irregular pines, and two hawks overhead, completing the circle of each other's figure eight, and a mound of ants by your shoe, going about their business, unaware of their wonder to you who are just shadow and foot. But you are not unaware, and when you think about it later, you realize this was the genesis, the beginning of a kind of prayer.

You say "a kind of prayer," even to yourself, because you are embarrassed—this communion being even more private than sex, which at least has a visible partner—and because it is nothing like the prayers you are used to hearing, which also embarrass you, where you ask God for something in return for a lifetime of devotion, or the ones where the prayerbook tells you what to say. You are embarrassed, too, because you are a rational person and take the world as it is presented to you. Last night you had a dream. In the dream you go to the door of your room in the retreat house, which is catercorner to the church. As you start turning the knob you realize that someone on the other side is turning it too. You are not frightened by this.

You open the door. A monk in a peaked hood is standing there. He asks if you would like help cleaning your room. You say no, you can do it yourself.

Prayer is ". . . no vain exercise of words, no mere repetition of certain sacred formulae, but the very movement itself of the soul, putting itself in a personal relation of contact with the mysterious power of which it feels the presence—it may be even before it has a name by which to call it," William James said in the lectures at Edinburgh that became *The Varieties of Religious Experience*.

You feel you have entered this relationship through your silence, as if it were a door, normally shut, which has come unhinged.

MASS. Just before the spectacle begins, the seating is rearranged. The priests, in white, take the stage; the monks leave the choir stalls and move forward to a crescent of chairs facing the altar. Behind them, on the left, is another set of chairs, six down and six across. Parishioners come out of the dark and assemble themselves there. The scripture is from the Book of Job, the part where Job, destroyed and afflicted, curses the day he was born. "Why is light given to him that is in misery, and life to the bitter in soul, who long for death, but it comes not," he cries. The hour's psalm, #87, recited, not sung, might be his refrain: "Wretched, close to death from my youth, I have borne

Your trials; I am numb. Your fury has swept down upon me; Your terrors have utterly destroyed me." Sad, terrible, poignant as this is, no one—not the priests or the monks, not the man in cowboy boots or the three Dominican nuns to his right—seems especially pained by it. Perhaps the Old Testament is easier to read if you know the New Testament is coming.

Father Felix celebrates the mass. He looks out of place enthroned on the wooden presider's chair, dressed in green vestments. But this is a different man. This is someone other than the mild fellow whose private words are hard to hear, so gingerly are they advanced, as if otherwise they might leave tracks and hasten erosion. He has been a monk at Gethsemani for almost forty years, cloistered throughout the Korean War, the Bay of Pigs, the assassinations, rock and roll, the moon walk, Vietnam, *Roe* v. *Wade*, music videos, everything. He looks remarkably young. He was twenty when he arrived in Kentucky from Cleveland after a year of premed studies at Case Western Reserve and a year of seminary. Those were the years when the rules of silence were more strictly enforced than they are today; to communicate, the monks developed their own sign language with seven hundred gestures. In those years, too, the monks slept together in a large dormitory on straw pallets. Now they have their own rooms. There were nearly four times as many brothers then, 272, and one of them was Thomas Merton.

Merton was a student at Columbia University in the 1930s when he converted to Catholicism and began considering—just considering—the priesthood. He taught for a while at St. Bonaventure's, wrote three novels and reams of poetry, worked with young children in Harlem, and finally found himself drawn not to the seminary but to the monastery. In December 1941, as America went to war against Japan, Merton packed his papers in boxes, distributed most of his possessions, and entered Gethsemani to become a monk. Committed to silence, he was nonetheless allowed to continue to write. Merton's autobiography, *The Seven Storey Mountain*, about his Augustinian journey to the monastic life, was published in 1948 and became a best-seller and something of a literary sensation and put Gethsemani, and the writer himself, on the map. Thirty-one books—poems, essays, aphorisms, Christology—followed, and with them scores of young men. Even now, more than twenty years after his death, he inspires pilgrims, if not postulants, to Gethsemani, who come to walk in the garden where he walked. Every day there is someone like the woman from Baltimore, who calls to ask which of Merton's books discusses Ionesco's *Rhinoceros* (*Conjectures of a Guilty Bystander*), or like the professor-priest from Florida, in Louisville to attend a wedding, who drives down to kneel at his grave.

Father Felix is the exception. He didn't read *The*

Seven Storey Mountain until after he became a novice. He never made it all the way through another of Merton's popular works, *Seeds of Contemplation*. He became a monk not because of books but because he "kind of liked the thought of a life of prayer, where everything is arranged to allow you to live in prayer." The arrangement he is talking about is the seven offices. Seven times a day, "you are pulled out of the busy-ness and given a fresh start, which permeates the whole day with a sense of values and a sense of presence." Monks at Gethsemani do four hours of manual or other nonspiritual work a day—in the bakery, in the fields (there are four hundred acres of farmland and a beef cattle herd), in the kitchen. For seventeen years, before becoming the retreat house chaplain, Father Felix worked in the infirmary, caring for sick and elderly monks. Labor, Silence, Prayer—day to day over forty years it has been pretty much the same. "It's a very good life," he says. "I'm lucky there is such a life."

His faith, like his sincerity, is quiet. Not tentative—quiet. He doesn't say "I believe this" or "I believe this and so should you." It is a faith so securely adhered to who he is that it *is* who he is—something on the order of Jung's "I don't believe, I know," where knowing is in fact being. When he says, "Basically, we're a bunch of men living together . . . this is really a pretty normal way of life," it is possible to see past the celibacy and the silence and agree. Or to look at these squarely and agree. It is possible because he leaves *no doubt*—making your own theological misgivings seem petty and dim—that he is called to God. Think of it this way: it's as if Father Felix appeared to be about six feet tall but in fact had four-inch lifts built into his shoes. Either he says there are lifts in his shoes or he doesn't, but either way you have to know they are there to believe him when he says that, actually, he is a relatively short guy.

TERCE. The monks, short and tall, white robed and black scapulared, singing, "You have laid down Your precepts to be obeyed with care. May my footsteps be firm to obey Your statutes." Singing, "Though I carry my life in my hands, I remember Your law." Singing, "Your will is wonderful indeed; therefore I obey it." This could be their anthem, so closely does it express their aspirations and their legacy. Obedience, poverty, and chastity, prescribed in his Holy Rule by Benedict of Nursia, patron saint of the Benedictines and Patriarch of Western Monks: this has been their way since the sixth century. But this is the twentieth century verging on the twenty-first, and poverty that is voluntary and chastity that is wholehearted go against the grain of our ambitions. Obedience is even more anathema—it's fingernails on the blackboard. After Locke and Tocqueville, after Hitler and Lenin, after Orwell and Huxley, we have come to equate authority with subjection and the escape from authority with freedom. A just, loving, honest, selfless, fair, dominant authority is unimaginable.

The monks sing, "I take delight in Your promise like one who finds a treasure. Lies I hate and detest, but Your law is my love." *What is this?* A priest who was a monk at Gethsemani explains: ". . . there is necessary for God's action on the human soul such a willingness to be at His disposal, almost as mere putty in His hands, that unless a man be willing to learn it by the hard discipline of obedience it may not be learned at all." Putty in His hands? This is exactly what we fear becoming in anybody's hands, God's or not, for such is the path to tyranny, cowardice, and to holocaust. In his Holy Rule St. Benedict decreed that monks were to obey their abbot as God's agent on earth. The abbot of twelve monasteries himself, Benedict must have recognized the benefits of institutional cohesion that this sort of suzerainty would have. But he also made obedience a school for faith, knowing it can be more difficult to abide by a man whose faults are apparent than by a God you cannot see. The unavoidable danger, though, is that in time the man will be feared and worshipped, not the God, and the putty will be molded into something ugly and grotesque, something on the order of the crowd in *The Brothers Karamazov* who fall away from Christ when he is arrested by the Grand Inquisitor. This fear—this is the way we think. We fear, with good reason, what submitting to authority will bring. Yet we fear, also with good reason, that we will—or you will—submit. We fear what will be lost—property, status, mobility, reason, ourselves.

The monks sing, "See how I love Your precepts; in Your mercy give me life." A nineteenth-century Catholic theologian suggests why, for monks, it is different: "By poverty [the monk] immolates his exterior possessions; by chastity he immolates his body; by obedience he completes the sacrifice and gives to God all that he holds as his own, his two most precious goods, his intellect and his will." Of course he is not afraid to submit to authority: he has nothing to lose. It is Dostoevsky, through the dying monk Father Zosima, who makes a far more audacious claim: submission is the yoke of liberty. "Obedience, fasting and prayer are laughed at, yet only through them lies the way to real, true freedom. I cut off my superfluous and unnecessary desires, I subdue my proud and wanton will and chastise it with obedience, and with God's help I attain freedom of spirit and with it spiritual joy."

The monks sing, "My soul obeys Your will and loves it dearly. I obey Your precepts and Your will; all that I do is before You."

SEXT. From here, a mile or so down a crusty farm track, the church bells could be wind chimes. The sign says: BULL IN FIELD, but there is no bull, just two woodchucks idling in my direction who dip into an overgrown spillway before our paths can cross. I try to name the trees—cyprus, walnut, pine, and cedar—until I feel like an inventory clerk, and not a very good one. But the trees lead me to water, to a pond fit snugly between two stands of conifers, where I sit. Silver fish vault through the surface into the air. Daredevils shot from cannons, they go up twice, once in reflection, and their splash, going up and coming down, is the only break in the stillness. It is possible to believe that this pond and these fish and those trees have been put here for me, because this is what I wanted to find, and that tomorrow, when someone else wanders through, there will be a den of bears or a tavern or a used-car lot—whatever they might be seeking.

It is possible to believe this because in certain expansive moods it is possible to believe anything. For instance, the other day, before lunch, I took three picture postcards from the retreat house reception desk, stuck them in my psalter, and promptly forgot about them. I know I forgot about them because when I went back into the sanctuary for sext they fell out of the book and scattered under the pew, and I had to crawl around to find them. I put them in the back of the psalter and forgot about them again. I know I forgot about them because after the service I met an older woman, a tourist, lost on the back stairs, who asked me if I knew where she could buy some postcards. I told her to follow me. About halfway to the retreat house I remembered the cards in the back of my book and turned and handed them to her. We were both amazed, as if they had just materialized there, which in a way they had.

NONE. The question is, where were they five or ten years ago, the young ones who sing, "How good and pleasant it is when brothers live in unity!" Were they happy at home, watching *Monday Night Football*, in love with some girl, desperate about their acne? Among the choir members is a young man in street clothes, with a full head of hair, thirty years old, from Colorado, who is about to join the order. He's an ordinary-looking fellow with no outward signs of cultural rebellion (for that is what this is). He is painfully inarticulate about why he wants to leave the material world, which I guess is how it should be. To be honest, it is sex I am interested in: how he can give it up. This seems the most obvious question, but I can't bring myself to ask it. Instead I tell myself: If I am not going to think that celibacy is unnatural, or that it is more unnatural than our relentless attention to sex, I've got to accept that I can't imagine being called to it, but can imagine that others are. Okay, but who are these others? How much easier to tell myself they are sexless, or contemptuous of women, or mortified. Much harder to think the opposite, because then it is possible to suffer their loss.

VESPERS. The walk I take, through the bottoms, over a rotting wooden bridge, along a gravel path, past five bales of hay and a pasture, ends in a cathedral of Virginia pine. I am resting on a rock, the sole parishioner besides the chipmunks and the robins, when I hear a voice—no, not the voice out of the whirlwind; it hasn't come to that. It is a male voice, singing. He sings one long note and stops. What he lacks in range he makes up in volume. I wonder where he is and how he has gotten there. Although I am two miles in from the road, I'm not scared; who can be frightened of someone out for a walk, singing? I think he may be a monk, practicing for vespers. After listening for a while, I walk to the edge of the woods, which borders a meadow, and spy him standing in the field. He is brown and white and chewing on grass.

Now it is our turn. We sing, "From Your dwelling You water the hills; earth drinks its fill of Your gift. You make the grass grow for the cattle and the plants to serve man's needs, that he may bring forth bread from the earth and wine to cheer man's heart; oil, to make his face shine and bread to strengthen man's heart." Palms up, palms down, palms up—the four women in front of me make a chain with their hands. In front of them is a woman who never stands with the crowd, and next to her a woman who rarely strays from her knees. I know these women by the back of their necks and by the grip of their fingers when the priest instructs us to turn to each other and say, "Peace be with you." I know them by the titles of the books they carry (*Life and Holiness, Meditation and Mental Process*) and by their comments in the guest register ("a closer walk with God," "getting in touch with God"). This is enough. We are a community of individuals in our solitude. I would rather not know their names.

In *Walden* Thoreau writes, "Men frequently say to me, 'I should think you would feel lonesome down there and want to be nearer to folks, rainy and snowy days and nights especially.' I am tempted to reply to such: . . . Why should I feel lonely? Is not our planet in the Milky Way? This which you put seems to me not to be the most important question. What sort of space is that which separates a man from his fellows and makes him solitary?" Here it is the space between words, the aureole of silence.

. . .

AFTER vespers Father Felix meets me in the graveyard. He is wearing a gray denim shirt, blue jeans, and hiking boots. He is taking me to Thomas Merton's hermitage. For Merton, silence was just the preamble to prayer. "For the first time in my life I am finding you, O solitude. I can count on the fingers of one hand the few short moments of purity, of neutrality, in which I have found you. Now I know I am coming to the day in which I will be free of words: their master rather than their servant, able to live without them if need be," he wrote in January 1950.

But this was not sufficient; he wanted to remove himself from the company of men and retreat into the woods. He wanted to become an anchorite. Merton had long been drawn to the Carthusians, a cenobitic order that was less a fellowship of brothers than a collection of ascetics, and if there had been a Carthusian monastery in America he might not have entered Gethsemani. Once he was there, though, he began asking to be allowed to follow in the tradition of the Desert Fathers and become a hermit. It is the hermitage the order built for him in 1959 that we are walking to.

When we get there, I am disappointed that it looks more like a suburban California tract house than the cave of the Essenes or Thoreau's cottage at Walden Pond. I notice the cables connecting it to the power grid. That's not all. Father Felix tells me Merton had a telephone. This strikes me as cheating. I want to believe he practiced virtues I am unwilling to. I want him to earn, in my currency, his sanctity.

In the end, though, this may be the value of monastic life for those of us on the other side of the gates, that it is a place where virtue, kindness, restraint, and craftsmanship are sought and where often they are attained. If we hold these religious men to a higher standard, it is because they hold themselves to it, and when they show it can be met, there are fewer excuses for the rest of us.

COMPLINE. We gather in the dusk. The triad shifts to a major key. We sing, "Fear Him; do not sin: ponder on your bed and be still. Make justice your sacrifice and trust in the Lord." Our voices are luminous. Light leaves through the window. Words shimmer on the page. We sing, "You will not fear the terror of the night nor the arrow that flies by day, nor the plague that prowls in the darkness, nor the scourge that lays waste at noon." Two candles are lit and placed on the easel in front of the picture of Mary. Their flame is reflected in the white of the monks' robes, which look themselves like tapers. We sing, "Upon you no evil shall fall, no plague approach where you dwell. For you has He commanded His angels, to keep you in all your ways." We sing, "The God that is, that was, and is to come, at the end of the ages." Now the candles are extinguished. Shoulder to shoulder, we stand in the dark. The bells are pealing. The church shakes underfoot. And then it stops.

. . .

I LEAVE before the sun comes up. The parking lot is crowded with pickup trucks that have farm plates. My headlights pick out four old women in wool skirts slowly walking toward the church. And then two more and a man coming up over the hill. And then another five people walking single file along the road. Are these the twelve disciples and is this Galilee? No—it is Sunday in the American croft. The man on the radio says, "If you need further assurance that Jesus is the Son of God and your personal savior, write to me at this address," and names some place in Missouri.

Maria

AT the Chris Brownlie AIDS hospice in Los Angeles, Maria Cruz has brought soup she made for her thirty-two-year-old son, José, who can no longer eat. He lies in bed curled toward the wall, a spindle of a man, nearly blind now. It is black bean soup and, untouched, it has grown cold on the tray beside him. His mother shrugs. In a little while she will put it in the refrigerator next to the paella and samosas she made him the week before, which sit on top of the chicken and rice she made the week before that. He cannot swallow, but he can at least smell.

Maria is holding my hand. I am here as a journalist to write about the hospice, but I cannot write because she has placed my hand inside hers and regards it as if it were a gift.

"I am very strong," she tells me. She speaks little English, though she has been here for thirty years, up from Guatemala, scrubbing other people's floors, ironing their shirts.

"I am strong in here." She points to her heart. "God is good. He gives me everything I ask for. People expect everything quickly, but God doesn't work that way." She lets go of my hand and drops down to the floor, this squat little woman in a blue housedress and ragged terry-cloth slippers, splays her fingers, and pats the carpet.

"My faith," she says, "is from here. It is deep in the ground." She asks me if I understand what she means. I say that I do, and I do, in a way, the easy way, the same way I understand when she says, "I love my son." But I do not have a son, and I do not have God in the same way as she, although it occurs to me that to have one might be to have the other.

"Pray for him," she says, nodding toward the bed when I get up to leave. I say I will, and what I pray for is his death.

. . .

THE friend's house I am staying at, high in the Hollywood Hills, has a picture window that frames the Los Angeles skyline. For the better part of a week I have come back from the hospice each evening and stood by that window, watching until the sun has gone down and the city is bathed in that alien orange glow of sodium vapor street lamps. This morning, unable to sleep, I see the sun overtake them.

I also see, on the table by the window, a book called *Vaclav Havel or Living in Truth*, with Havel's face on the cover. It is a younger face than the one that has become so familiar these days, a face that does not yet spell the address of every prison he's been in. I pick it up reflexively, as though it were a newspaper left on the seat of a train by the passenger before me, and leaf through it aimlessly.

In fact, the book has been there all week, and I have avoided it. What could a man of ideas have to say about living or truth that wouldn't be an abstraction? In the hospice, in the corridor of death, there is no time for that which is obscure. It is a place where people *have no choice* but to live in truth.

The essay I read is called "Politics and Conscience." I read it twice and then, compelled, I take out my notebook, and under the heading "Maria Cruz," on the lines where I could not take any notes, I begin to copy it down. I find that in it is a more apt description of her—and of the hospice—than anything I might have written in its place: "In this world, categories like justice, honor, treason, friendship, infidelity, courage, or empathy have a wholly tangible content, relating to actual persons and important for actual life. At the basis of this world are values which are simply there, perennially, before we ever speak of them, before we reflect upon them and inquire about them. It owes its internal coherence to something like a 'prespeculative' assumption that the world functions and is generally possible at all only because there is something beyond its horizon, something beyond or above it that might escape our understanding and our grasp but, for just that reason, firmly grounds this world, bestows upon it its order and measure, and is the hidden source of all the rules, customs, commandments, prohibitions, and norms that hold within it."

Reading this over, I think of Ken at the opposite

end of the hall from José, six feet tall, 117 pounds, riddled with lymphoma, losing his sight. "I've come to terms with why I'm here," he told me one afternoon. "My mother and brother haven't. 'You should put your faith in God,' they keep telling me. I do believe in God. I know it's up to each person, how you approach Him. But they still think they can ask Him to make me well." And I think of Tony, a former hospice resident who is well enough now to volunteer at Chris Brownlie twice a week, and his conviction that he is the one who is going to beat this disease, that he is the one who will heal himself. And I think of Maria, patiently reading her Bible with one eye, keeping watch over her son with the other.

She is not there when I next return to the hospice. Someone thinks she has gone home for a few hours, to feed her cats and, I imagine, to cook for José. It strikes me that it is not some fantasy that inspires her to prepare meals that he will never eat but something born, as Havel might say, of a "prespeculative" realism. The food, her vigilance—this is what she can give to him. This is what she has always given to him. And he, lying there, though inert, gives back to her in return the dailiness of their lives—that which gives love its openings.

. . .

SOME years ago I was enamored of a clever young man who had worked out an entire system to prove that marriage was stupid. I don't think he actually used the word *stupid*, but that was the gist of it. Nor did he use the word *marriage*. Rather, he called it "the retreat to the kitchen." What is most onerous about the retreat to the kitchen, he argued, is that it preoccupies people with the trivial necessities of life, reducing their concerns to "the buying of bread," which prevents them from devoting their energies to working out the details of, say, unified field theory or literary deconstruction.

I retreated to the kitchen with someone else but haven't bought a loaf of bread since. Instead, I've bought yeast and flour and honey and eggs, and once a week I spend the morning baking. Strictly speaking, I suppose you could say I do this solely for my husband's benefit since I am allergic to wheat and cannot eat the bread I make. But like José, I can smell it. And like his mother, I just do it—thoughtlessly—because it is what I do in this life my husband and I are making together, because it is one of the ways in which this life is made.

I left the Chris Brownlie hospice before José's mother got back, so I don't know what she brought him that day. Back home I might have been doing anything— petting the dog, planning our garden, kneading dough—when he died.

Telling
the Truth

IT is Friday night in Snacks, Indiana, and Karen Bell is sitting in the dark in her daughter Becky's bedroom listening to the Lynyrd Skynyrd Band sing "Freebird." It's been two years since Becky died, and by now the mother knows the words as well as the daughter ever did. If you meet Karen Bell she will play Becky's favorite song for you, quietly singing along: "If I leave here tomorrow, would you still remember me? I must be traveling on now . . . cause I'm free as a bird now, and this bird you'll never change. . . . But please don't take it so badly, cause the Lord knows I'm to blame. If I stay here with you now, things just couldn't be the same." Karen Bell will play the song, and for a moment you will glimpse the depth of a mother's grief.

· · ·

BECKY BELL did not have to die. Her family knows it, and so do their friends and neighbors in suburban Indianapolis. They know it now. Only she knew it then, in the summer of 1988. But what is death to a teenager? Anyway, it wasn't death on her mind that summer; it was life. Becky Bell was pregnant and she didn't want to be, and if she hadn't lived in Indiana, that might have been that. She would have gone to a doctor, had an abortion, finished high school, gone to college, gotten married, raised a family. But it didn't happen that way. Indiana requires girls under eighteen to get the consent of one parent before they can have an abortion, and Becky Bell didn't want her mother and father to know she was pregnant. She couldn't bring herself to tell them. And so she died, three weeks after her seventeenth birthday, of something almost no one in America dies from anymore—a botched abortion, an abortion doctors say she may have performed on herself.

. . .

BEFORE their daughter died, Bill and Karen Bell had no idea that girls in Indiana do not have the same access to abortion as women over eighteen. They didn't know that in 1976, just three years after the Supreme Court legalized abortion in *Roe* v. *Wade*, it ruled that a teenager's right to privacy when deciding whether or not to have an abortion was weaker than an adult woman's, and that a state could legitimately require her parents' participation in that decision. They were unaware that Indiana is one of thirty-one states with laws requiring parental consent or parental notification, and that it is among the eleven states that actually enforce those laws. What they didn't know, in other words, was that if their teenager got pregnant and wanted an abortion, one of them would have to sign a piece of paper saying it was okay. "Why should I have known about parental consent?" Karen Bell asks. "I was home with my girl and my boy. We were a good family. We talked. It didn't concern us."

These days, it seems, parental consent is the only thing that concerns the Bells. Although the minister at Becky's funeral told the mourners how she had died, it wasn't until the pain had settled some that the Bells went public with their story, and with their contempt for laws like the one they hold responsible for their daughter's death. They have been on the CBS *Morning News* and the Geraldo Rivera show, been profiled in *People* magazine, seen a memorial to their daughter temporarily erected on the mall in Washington, and testified before the legislatures of seven states considering parental consent or parental notification laws. The Bells aren't lobbyists, they're missionaries. They're good at what they do, too, this preaching to the unconverted, to those who believe that laws requiring parental consent or notification for minors' abortions are beneficial because they force teenagers to talk to their parents and because they give parents some control over their children. Two hours after Bill Bell addressed a group of lawmakers in Wisconsin, for example, the committee sponsoring that state's parental consent bill tossed it out.

. . .

I FIRST meet the Bells in the rotunda of the Florida Statehouse in Tallahassee. It's an out-of-town tryout for Bill, who is on the verge of quitting his job as a fax machine salesman to work full-time as a pitchman for The Fund for the Feminist Majority. The Bells are a physically striking couple—it fits that she was Homecoming Queen and he a high school basketball star. What doesn't fit is that this man, who can often be found drinking beer and talking sports with his buddies at the VFW Hall, and his wife, who, leaning over to greet a legislative aide whispers, "Shalimar," and who *subscribes* to the *National Enquirer*, are the vanguard of opposition to laws that many dedicated abortion rights advocates find acceptable. These are the folks Ronald Reagan was talking about when he extolled traditional family values, and these are the folks who voted for him. Bill Bell is a registered Republican, and if there were a GOP card to carry, he would. As he is fond of saying, "I sat with Molly Yard, the president of the National Organization for Women, at dinner and said, 'Molly, I wouldn't be surprised if abortion was the only issue on which you and I agree.' "

It is NOW that has flown Karen and Bill down to Florida, put them up for a night at the Hilton, and sent them out early the next morning to talk to politicians NOW believes will benefit from hearing the story of a girl who was so afraid of disappointing her parents by telling them she was pregnant that she resorted to a means of ending her pregnancy that killed her. Although the Florida Supreme Court recently overturned a parental consent law, certain legislators are threatening to resurrect it, and it is this prospect that drives the Bells up and down the statehouse hallways as if it were the Speedway back home. At 2:15 they have been at it for five hours, and they are only halfway through the day. They introduce themselves to Senator Jeanne Malchon, a Democrat they have been told is a "friend."

"We're here from Indianapolis," Bill Bell tells Malchon, "because our seventeen-year-old daughter, Becky, died of an illegal abortion."

Having cast his line, he waits. The senator doesn't say a word. Bell tries again.

"Our daughter would still be alive today if we'd lived in a state that didn't require teenagers to get parental consent for abortions," he says. This time Malchon takes the bait, and suddenly she's the fish that won't get away, launching into her stump speech on abortion, oblivious to the fact that the Bells live maybe nine hundred miles shy of her district.

Bill and Karen listen politely. A friend's a friend.

"Everyone is pro-life, everyone is anti-abortion," the senator says. "Abortion is an unfortunate solution to an unfortunate problem. Sometimes a straight line is not the shortest route between two points." When the senator runs out of these pleasantries, she stands up, dismissing her audience. "I'm sorry about your personal tragedy," she says as the Bells walk out the door.

· · ·

SEPTEMBER 16, 1988, the day Becky Bell died, about 2,825 teenage girls got pregnant in the United States. It was the same the next day, when young people and their parents lined the sidewalk in front of the funeral home where her body lay, standing three-deep in the rain to pay their last respects. These were typical days that add up to a typical year of well over one million pregnancies to girls eighteen and younger, the highest teenage pregnancy rate in the industrial world. About 80 percent of these pregnancies are unplanned; about half end in abortion. According to researchers from the American Psychological Association and the National Institute of Child Health and Development, teenagers who choose to abort their pregnancies have "a stronger sense of the future" than the ones who choose to have and keep their babies. It was into this group, ironically, the one that looked ahead, that Becky Bell fell.

Like her parents, Becky Bell was unaware of Indiana's parental consent requirement until it had something to do with her. That was two months before she died, when the Planned Parenthood counselor sat her down, told her she was pregnant, and began to lay out her options. "Dear Mom and Dad," Becky wrote to her parents around this time in a note they found much later, in her purse, "I wish I could tell you everything, but I can't. I have to deal with it myself. I can do it and I love you."

. . .

BILLY BELL eases his four-by-four pickup off the highway into the dark precincts of downtown Indianapolis. He is blond, like the sister who was two years younger than he, conventionally handsome, mildly distracted. We have been driving around, taking in the sights. Pike Township, where the Bells live, used to be pleasant, flat farmland. It is still flat, but scores of new subdivisions have gone up where corn used to grow, and they give the landscape a forced, desperate expression, like people at a party who are trying just a little too hard to be happy. Billy mentions that since his sister died he often finds himself driving his truck, talking to her as if she were sitting where I am. People look in the window, he says, and see his mouth moving, and notice he is alone.

"My mother's whole mission in life was to raise us," he says later on. We are stopped at a traffic light during a cloudburst, and the image of the rain, beading on the windshield, is projected, magnified, onto his face, and for a minute it looks as if he were crying. But he isn't crying, doesn't cry. "Becky was my mother's princess. She was the girl who could do no wrong. She couldn't live up to it. She couldn't go to my parents when she was in trouble, not because they wouldn't help her, but because she didn't want them to know she wasn't a princess."

"It's true, if Becky came to us and said she was pregnant, I would have been mad. I admit it," Karen says. "I would've thought about what the neighbors would say, and I would've told her she had ruined her life. She knew that I'd have said that, but I'd also have done everything possible for her."

. . .

BECKY BELL couldn't tell her parents she was pregnant and wanted an abortion because she was afraid of what they would think of her. For Mary Moe, a pregnant seventeen-year-old from Roxbury, Massachusetts, I met in the Middlesex County Courthouse in Cambridge—and *thousands* of other girls—it is the same. Mary, the daughter of a single mother, is an articulate high school senior who aspires to go to music school. This is her second pregnancy. A year earlier, when Mary was pregnant for the first time, her mother angrily consented to an abortion. She also called Mary a murderer. So did her boyfriend. So did friends in the housing project where she lives, many of whom have children themselves. Last time, when friends there found out she was pregnant they urged her to have the baby; her kids could play with their kids, they said.

When they heard she had had an abortion, they turned on her. But it was her mother, who refused to talk to her for weeks afterward, who hurt her most. Afraid of antagonizing her this time, Mary has arranged with a lawyer, referred to her by Planned Parenthood, to appeal to a judge for a waiver of the consent requirement in order to avoid involving her mother at all.

For her appointment with the judge Mary has dressed in lavender cotton pants and a matching sweater. The outfit is neat but casual—she couldn't risk arousing her mother's suspicions—and now that she is in court she is worried that it is not dressy enough, and she will make a bad impression on the judge, and he will deny her the abortion. In the elevator on the way up to the judge's chambers Mary thinks she is going to be sick. Her lawyer, whom she met for the first time only fifteen minutes ago, holds her hand.

In his chambers Superior Court Judge Joseph Mitchell delivers a rapid-fire round of questions to the girl: How far along is she, what grade is she in, can she describe the risks of abortion? Satisfied that Mary is competent to give informed consent, the judge approves her petition and sends her on her way. The entire interview has taken less than five minutes. It is Judge Mitchell's 265th judicial bypass hearing this year and his 265th approval. It is no wonder the lawyers seek him out.

Judge Mitchell is not only sympathetic toward the

pregnant teenagers who come into his chambers; he believes that it is wrong to require them to come there at all. Abortion should be solely a matter between a pregnant woman and her physician, he says. This opinion, which is shared by few of Judge Mitchell's colleagues, is why he alone hears about half of the state's nine hundred judicial bypass petitions. His colleagues, meanwhile, have been known to ask pregnant teenagers in open court why they can't keep their knees together, and to invent game-show hypotheticals to "test" the minors' maturity. (During one hearing, according to a lawyer who was there, a judge is reported to have asked a fifteen-year-old girl how she would spend a thousand dollars if suddenly someone gave it to her. "I'd put it in the bank," she told him. "No," he said, "you have to spend it." "I don't want to spend it," she said, "I want to save it." "You can't," said the judge. "All right," she said, "I'd take a vacation in the Caribbean." "The Caribbean?" the judge asked. "Well, what if you had the choice between a week in the Caribbean, a week in Europe, and two weeks in California, which would you choose?" "I don't speak French," the girl replied. That matter seemed to end there, but later, when the judge was reviewing her school transcripts he noticed she had studied Spanish. "Spanish?" he asked her. "Are you sure you don't want to reconsider going to Europe?")

. . .

THE judicial bypass procedure was available to Becky
Bell in Indiana, since Indiana, like all states that require parental consent, must also provide an alternative
way for girls to get permission for the abortion from
a neutral third party, usually a judge. But Indiana has
no Judge Mitchell, and only a handful of waivers have
been granted, not one of them in Indianapolis. "Go
face to face with a judge to ask him to let me have an
abortion? I could never do that," says Becky's child-
hood friend, Ann McDougal. Apparently, neither
could Becky.

It has been argued, in the courts and in the press,
that parental consent and parental notification laws are
intended to punish young women for getting pregnant,
for having sex. It has been argued that these laws say
to teenage girls, "Okay, have your cake and eat it too,
all of it, even if it makes you sick, because you were
the one who piled it on your plate." Listen, for instance, to lawyers for the State of Ohio explaining to
the Supreme Court in 1989 why the Ohio parental
notification law did not need a bypass procedure: "The
state notifies parents when a minor child is charged as
a truant, a delinquent, an unruly child, or a traffic
offender. While parents could react with hostility to
the knowledge that their child was acting outside the
law, just as they could react hostilely to their daughter's

pregnancy, such a possibility does not mandate the necessity for a bypass procedure." One wonders, though, if Mary Moe had skipped school for a month, would she have gone to extremes to prevent her mother from finding out? If Becky Bell had run a red light, would she have been mortally afraid of her parents?

· · ·

WHAT went on in the two months between the pregnancy diagnosis and Becky's death remains something of a mystery. She was confused, her friends say, indecisive about everything except her decision not to talk to her parents. She was pretty sure she wanted an abortion, but not completely sure. She thought she might go down to Kentucky, seventy miles away, a state where teenagers can end their pregnancies without their parents' knowledge, but then she didn't go. In August she went to Florida on vacation with her parents. Her bikini didn't give her away. When she got home she told different friends different things. To Robin Peters, a co-worker at Cub Foods, where she worked part-time as a cashier, she said she had gone to Kentucky and had an abortion. To Eric Merrill, a schoolmate, she said she had had an abortion in Indiana and her mother had been with her. To Heather Clark, her best friend, she confided that she was still pregnant, that time was running out, that she had to do something.

Odds are, Becky Bell did not find her way to a back-alley abortionist in the weeks before she died, because it is unlikely that she could have found one. Most were put out of business by the Supreme Court in 1973 when they legalized abortion in *Roe* v. *Wade*. Delbert Culp, director of Indianapolis Planned Parenthood, speculates that "if there were someone in town doing illegal abortions, we'd most likely have picked it up on the grapevine. I've never heard that, and you'd think that we would have at least heard a rumor." The other reason why a back-alley abortionist was probably not responsible is statistical: Becky's was the first and last case of death by septic abortion that the Marion County coroner had recorded in years. If a hack were at work, his signature would have been seen more than once. Even now, years after the fact, the coroner, Dr. Dennis Nicholas, says he remembers the case of Becky Bell because it was so unusual, so ahistorical. "It used to be that I'd get deaths from criminal abortions, but that was back before abortions were legalized and became easily available. I just don't see them anymore." Indiana is bordered by states that don't require parental consent; teenagers who want abortions can get them there, legally, safely.

How Becky Bell came by an illegal abortion is anyone's guess, the coroner says, now that the expert witness is dead. It's his belief that someone—perhaps Becky herself—introduced something (a knitting needle, a piece of wire?) unsterile into her uterus in order to get it to contract and cause a miscarriage. The unsterile instrument had another effect, too. It led to an infection that traveled through her bloodstream and settled in her lungs, causing the pneumonia that ultimately killed her.

. . .

BILL BELL had been sick with the flu that first week of September, so the next week, when his daughter complained of similar symptoms, he and his wife had no reason to think it was anything out of the ordinary. Becky was sick but not so sick that on Monday, September 12, she couldn't go to work at the supermarket or to Ritter High School, where she was in the second week of her junior year, having spent her first two years of high school at Pike High, where her mother, father, and brother preceded her. She had been feeling ill for days, ever since she had come back from a party the Saturday before, groggy, complaining that someone had laced her Coke with something. She had gone to the party with a girl friend who, Becky told her mother before she left, was having problems—maybe she'd spend the night at the girl's house. She didn't, though. Becky got home sometime after 1 A.M., said she felt funny, and went straight to bed.

The next day, Sunday, still feeling out of sorts, Becky went to work at Cub Foods, where she fainted.

On Monday, at Ritter, she told friends she was sick, and cried when she told them. On Tuesday she stayed home. When her parents asked if she wanted to see a doctor, she said she didn't. By Wednesday Becky was running a fever. On Thursday it spiked at 103 degrees. When her parents again suggested going to the doctor, she again said no. They didn't push it—the fever was breaking. She didn't tell them how it hurt to breathe.

Becky started to bleed, vaginally, Friday morning. She told her mother that she had gotten her period, but she was so weak that she asked Karen to escort her into the bathroom. She came out an hour later, bleeding heavily, wheezing. This time, when her father said something about going to the doctor, she didn't object.

It was late afternoon by the time the doctor could see her. He listened to her lungs, took an X ray, determined that she had pneumonia, and sent her immediately to the hospital. Her lungs were full of fluid. The fluid was like a rising tide. Seven hours later, unable to breathe against it, she died.

· · ·

THE first inkling Bill and Karen had that Becky's was not a straightforward case of pneumonia came not long after she was admitted to the hospital. They had gone out to get a quick dinner, and when they came back, a doctor ushered them into a conference room before they had had a chance to see their daughter, and shut the door. He told them that while they were gone Becky had stopped breathing for a time, that she was unconscious and in the intensive care unit. But that wasn't necessarily the worst of the bad news. "I'm going to have to break Becky's confidence and tell you that she's pregnant," Karen recalls the doctor saying, "and I'm not sure we're going to be able to save the baby." Karen also recalls getting hysterical and yelling something about how she didn't care about saving that baby, it was *her* baby they should save.

The second inkling came early the next morning, just a few hours after Becky's death, when Dr. Nicholas, the coroner, called. Yes, he said, Becky *had been* pregnant, but at the time of death there were no "retained products of conception"—in other words, there was no fetus. A few hours later the coroner's office called back to say the death was being ruled a "criminal abortion."

. . .

WHEN Karen and Bill Bell meet with legislators who favor mandating parental involvement, Karen Bell invariably asks, "Where is the boy, where is the boy in all of this—that is what I want to know." It is an aimless, unanswerable question, even for herself. She doesn't really know what happened to the boy who was the father of Becky's child. He didn't go to the funeral, didn't get in touch afterward. He had been unwelcome at the Bells' for months before Becky died; Bill Bell, especially, thought that the boy, who had recently dropped out of school, was a bad influence on Becky. The day she got pregnant she had seen him on the sly, which may have been another reason why she could not tell her parents what had happened.

"She was sort of forced to rebel," Billy Bell says of his sister. "We were such a close family."

Her sophomore English teacher, Ann Booth, puts it another way. "Becky was going through that wild phase everyone goes through," she says. "She was a little off-center for a moment. I think she would have come back to the middle. She just didn't have time."

. . .

IT is early evening at the Tallahassee airport. Bill and Karen Bell are in the lounge, waiting for Congressman Bill Nelson. The congressman is running for governor, and he wants to hear what the Bells have to tell him. He's arranged to fly up from Miami before they take off for Indianapolis. Earlier in the day they met with the man who will eventually beat him, former senator Lawton Chiles. "He wanted to talk about compromise language," Bill says. "I don't understand compromise language. How do you compromise with someone's life?"

Nelson's plane is late, and as they wait, Karen and Bill run down the day's scorecard. They are not sure they changed anyone's mind, but they are satisfied they pitched a good game. Karen relates a conversation she had with Rep. George Crady, a pro-choice Democrat who supports parental consent, that still disturbs her.

"He's got five daughters, pretty, with dark hair," she says. "He told us that he knew that if his girls were in trouble, they'd tell him. When I was leaving his office, I said, 'I envy you your daughters, sir, and I hope they can come to you when they're in trouble.' He said, 'I know they would come to me.' I said, 'I knew our daughter would come to us, too.' "

Secret Beach

IN my appointment book for March that year are the notes I took during lunch with S. at a Los Angeles restaurant. "Snorkel at Shipwreck. Tropical Taco. Gaylord's (late). Brickoven Pizza (local hangout)." As the calendar shows, I was going to Hawaii the next day, from the airport at Oahu directly to Kauai, the green island. Kauai was his favorite island, S. said, and Hawaii his favorite place in the world. He had been there eighteen times. This was my first trip. S. said he was jealous. I knew what he meant. Years before, in college, where we met in a short story class, S. had delivered the wisdom that you can only fall in love for the first time once.

The restaurant where we were to have lunch was in a yellow clapboard house that stood out in the middle of downtown Hollywood like a man in chinos at a formal dinner. S. was late, and while I waited, I read scripts from the cops-and-robbers TV show another college friend was producing for one of the networks. That morning I had sat in on one of the show's story meetings ("Why don't we have the fucking jogger run past and turn and fucking blow her away?" one writer said. "What about the fucking bodyguard?" another writer, who happened to be her husband, said. "So

how about a fucking bomb and get them out like that?"
the first writer said) and had gone away with a stack
of party favors. By this time I had been in L. A. a week,
interviewing people at the Chris Brownlie AIDS hospice, and the scripts' violence seemed purposeful to
me. Everyone died to advance the plot.

S. rushed in the door and stopped short, looking
for me. This rushing was very familiar. Even if I didn't
recognize him, I would recognize *it*. And the odd thing
was, I didn't recognize him, really. His hair, which I
remembered being thick and the color of cedar, was
sparse and the color of pine. And his frame had shrunk.
It was as if the photographer, having first printed the
picture at eight by ten, had pulled in the borders by
a third.

My friend caught sight of me, waved, and smiled.
He was so skinny that when he did, his face folded
into long gullies on either side of his mouth, like
spillways beside a stream. When he moved toward me,
my body started to hum the way I imagine a divining
rod does in the presence of water. He has it, I thought.
He has it too.

But no, I must be mistaken. A week at the hospice
has warped my perceptions. He can't have it. He's my
friend. This is aging—what happens when you haven't
seen each other in four years. His clothes fit, he had
a job, he went to the office. He wouldn't be laughing
if he had it. He wouldn't be going on CNN in forty

minutes for a live interview. I tell him about the hospice, I give him openings. *His clothes fit.* He tells me how the magazine he writes for is due for another AIDS story, and he's thinking of writing about the family of the actor who played Starsky on *Starsky and Hutch* because all of them except Starsky have AIDS. We talk about Hutch's failed recording career. He picks at his food. Of course he's so thin.

S. takes me to CNN and leaves me in the green room with Ricardo Montalban. Ricardo and I watch him on the monitor as the interviewer in Atlanta asks my friend about the impact of home video on the movies. The interviewer asks the question once, and then, after S. has answered it, asks the same question again. S. slides to the edge of laughter but manages to hang on and pretend the guy has asked him something completely different. The TV gives him half his weight back. He looks fit. Of course he's not sick.

Ricardo Montalban, on the other hand, looks like hell. He's got a body cast of pancake makeup on because he's between shoots. After we've been sitting alone in the green room for five minutes, saying nothing, he apologizes to me for his appearance. I'm not sure of the etiquette, so I tell him I don't mind.

Back at S.'s house we giggle about this. We eat jelly beans and discuss whether or not the McMartins are guilty of molesting children at their preschool. We talk about our college friends who are having babies, that kind of thing. He tells me more about Kauai, about a beach there I should go to. I ask how to get to it. He can't remember the precise directions and advises me to ask when I get there. "What's its name?" I say. "It doesn't have a proper name," S. says. He and his friends call it secret beach. He's sure I'll find it, though. I say I'll send a postcard when I do.

. . .

"[S]ECRECY hides far more than what is private," Sisela Bok has written. "A private garden need not be a secret garden; a private life is rarely a secret life. Conversely, secret diplomacy rarely concerns what is private, any more than do arrangements for a surprise party. . . ." But what about where the private life is a secret garden and it has always been off-limits to you? And what if you respect those limits because you think you know what's inside them? It's you who would be keeping secrets then, and that's how it was with me and S. But maybe he knew I knew, so maybe there were no secrets, just the pretense of secrecy, and maybe what was not gone into, not said, is what let us talk.

. . .

I DIDN'T go to Kauai after all. My husband met me at the airport in Honolulu with tickets to Maui, and within two hours we were sitting on the porch of a man who had four hundred different kinds of palms on his property. That night we celebrated our anniversary watching the moon rise over Haleakala. Clouds rolled around the rim of the crater like basketballs going into the hoop on a slow-motion video replay.

After that we drove, under the bamboo thatch of the Hana Highway, along cliffs above black sand beaches, through the world's only tropical drive-through botanical garden, following the tail of a tropic bird, narrow as the needle of a compass. We decided to go to the Big Island of Hawaii. The lava was flowing at Kalapana, and we took out reporters' notebooks and strapped on cameras and convinced the local Civil Defense officer to let us see the place where it dropped into the ocean. While he was recruiting someone to take us, we went down the road and sat in a church decorated with elaborate murals of the priest who came to Hawaii to save the lepers and ended up getting the disease himself.

A native guide led us over live lava fields. The air smelled like rotting eggs. Heat stabbed our feet. We took pictures of steam geysers, of a red sea of magma charging through the filament, of exotic arabesques of hardened stone. The sky was an infallible sky-blue. Sight-seeing planes made pass after pass through the steam and skimmed the boiling ocean. Our guide kept urging us to move closer to the molten lava. My husband kept on going. I stood still and my sneakers melted.

About a month later the lava took a sharp left turn and swallowed fourteen houses, a store, a church, and the Civil Defense station where we met our guide. The Painted Church was left standing because parishioners had uprooted it and hauled it away. I read about this operation in the magazine S. worked for before I noticed he had made his nineteenth trip to Hawaii. Of course he wasn't sick.

In New York City around the same time, I mentioned to a friend the sense of distortion I experienced seeing S., how he looked so much like the young men in the hospice I had been interviewing. Trust your instincts, she said.

Not long afterward I told this same friend how sorry I was not to have written to S. when I had the chance. That's what death's about, she said. Regret.

. . .

IN the letter I regret not writing I would have urged S., if he was sick, to quit his job and write his novel. (He was a dazzling writer of fiction, but for a person who wanted to keep others off his secret beach, journalism offered defensive breakers.) I would have tried to win him over by quoting Grace Paley, whose writing he adored: "The kids, the kids! Though terrible troubles hang over them, such as the absolute end of the known world quickly by detonation or slowly through the easygoing destruction of natural resources, they are still, even now, optimistic, humorous, and brave. In fact, they intend enormous changes at the last minute."

. . .

I FOUND out S. had died when I was reading the *New York Times* one morning at breakfast. If only I had known he was sick, I told myself. But I had, hadn't I? How much knowledge do you have to have before you know? If only he had told me, I said to myself. What then? Anyway, he wasn't going to tell me. That was the point.

"I don't think it's right to complain about the character of the dying or start hustling all their motives into the spotlight like that," says a character in another Grace Paley story, called "Friends." "Isn't it amazing enough, the bravery of that private inclusive intentional community?"

It is amazing. It is even amazing enough. And what is amazing is that it is not dying that joins them but something quite the opposite. We sat in the living room, two old friends talking. S. was dying but didn't mention it. Looking back, I think he didn't mention it for his own sake, not for mine—so he could have afternoons like that, easy and sweet. Before this, I understood it took courage to admit that you had AIDS. Afterward I understood that sometimes there is courage—optimistic, humorous, brave—in silence, as well.

. . .

In the same Grace Paley story, "Friends," one character observes, "Abby isn't the only kid who died. What about that great guy, remember Bill Dalrymple—he was a non-cooperator or a deserter? And Bob Simon. They were killed in automobile accidents. Matthew, Jeannie, Mike. . . . The tendency, I suppose, is to forget."

At lunch in L.A. that day, S. asked me if I knew anyone who had died of AIDS. I said I didn't. (He must have known, then, that he would be the first.) He said he knew so many that he had lost track. "I used to write their names in a notebook when they died, but then there were so many I couldn't keep up with it," he said. "Then I couldn't remember who was alive and who was dead. So I started writing down their names again."

. . .

Enormous Changes at the Last Minute. S. gave me that book for my twenty-second birthday. In it, he wrote, "You'll never be immune, but you should be used to living now." I think I would have put that in my letter, too.

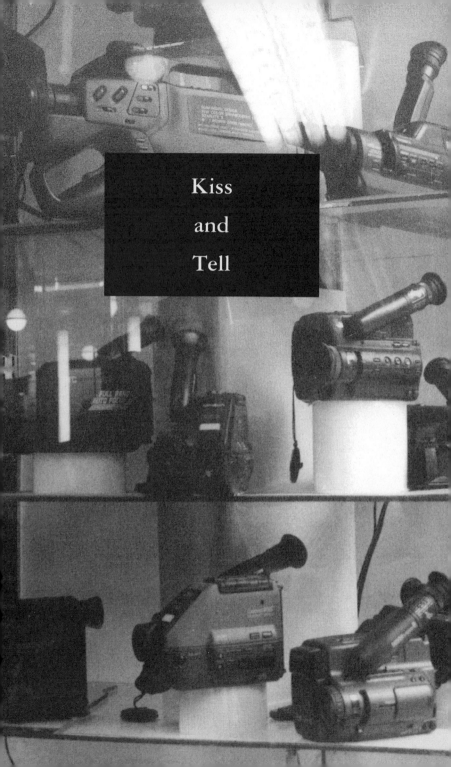

Kiss
and
Tell

THE man I am talking to reminds me of the insurance salesman who knocked on the back door a few years ago and asked if I knew the date of my next accident. We are in his office on the eightieth floor of the Empire State Building. The name of the man's company is SPYTECH. His name is Ed Sklar. He is making me nervous.

"Let me ask you a question," Mr. Sklar says. I have just inquired about his clientele, who they might be, the people who buy the briefcase tape recorders and infrared cameras he sells. Mr. Sklar moves forward in his chair, as if we're going to have a tête-à-tête—that is, as if we're going to touch heads. I can't help but get a good look at him. I'd guess he's about fifty, with kids in college and a house in New Jersey—a good provider but with money worries, maybe.

"Let me ask you a question," he says again. "Do you trust your husband?"

I grin at him reflexively. "Of course I do," I say. I want to say more, but I'm afraid to sound as though I'm protesting too much, so I don't.

Mr. Sklar leans way back and gives me a good, long, hard look. I don't move, except my face: I retract my grin. I am a deer caught in the web of light between the high beams.

"Well, a lot of women don't," he says.

Ed Sklar trades on marital infidelity and employee theft the way options brokers deal in soy and corn futures. Except in Mr. Sklar's business there are no droughts. Businesses lose $60 billion a year to employee theft, he tells me. What price adultery? This is not a rhetorical question. Divorce lawyers are paid to ask it, knowing that they will be paid even more if they can show incontrovertible evidence of the affair—a picture of a man in bed with his paramour, say, or, better yet, a *moving* picture.

Ed Sklar will outfit you, or your lawyer, or the private investigator you or your lawyer has hired, with the riggings to embark on this voyage of discovery: a 35mm camera that takes pictures in the dark or one that can "see" through curtains, a voice-activated tape recorder sewn into the lining of a leather purse, a video camera lodged in the belly of Garfield the Cat, which is one of two hundred varieties of hidden cameras he makes. Of the lot, Mr. Sklar's favorite is one where the camera is concealed in the control panel of a 40-inch Sony Trinitron. In his newspaper ads he calls it "the TV that watches you." But it doesn't watch you unless you are particularly curious about what you look like when you are staring at the Cosbys or *America's Most Wanted*. It watches your lover, your baby-sitter, your business partner, and anyone else whose shadow might fall across its screen when you're not around. When I wonder aloud about the likelihood of one's wife carrying on with the milkman in her marital bed, four feet from the television set, Mr. Sklar shrugs. "You'd be surprised," he says.

When I meet Ed Sklar, he is on the backside of the crest of a small wave of celebrity that has included appearances on the *Phil Donahue Show*, NBC *News*, CBS *News Nightwatch, Nine Broadcast Plaza*, the CBS *Morning Show* with Kathleen Sullivan. (This is before his second wave—selling gas masks to North Americans during the Gulf War.) Mr. Sklar has been in demand because Congress is considering a bill to require consent before a person can be videotaped. Such a bill, one assumes, would be bad for companies like SPYTECH, but that is not why Mr. Sklar is against it. He is against it because it would be bad for the country. "Any individual who wishes to tape another will need to inform that individual first," I read on the second page of his nine-page press kit. "In many cases this will defeat the purpose of the taping. It seems logical that one will not be as free with his/her speech if they are notified that they are being taped."

I also read, on the same page, what I construe to be SPYTECH's mission statement: "A perfect society would arguably deserve the right to total privacy at all costs. Unfortunately, our society is less than perfect, and where do we draw the fine line between when it is okay to violate a person's privacy and when it is not? Some critics believe that high-tech surveillance has gone too far—that George Orwell's vision of 1984 has come to life." The three sentences strike me as a kind of haiku: a little verbose, maybe, but inscrutable.

It is 1990 when I read this, six years after the events in Orwell's novel are supposed to have taken place, and it's as easy to be complacent about incursions into our private lives as it is to be outraged—it's just one more issue on the agenda at the moment, a moment characterized in part by our luxury in choosing which issues we'll be interested in, as if we were philanthropists and they our favorite charities. There aren't videophones yet, but there is caller ID; there isn't a central national data bank, but the average American appears in thirty-nine government data bases and forty or so private-sector files, and his name passes through and between them about five times a day; there are laws against wiretapping, but they do not cover cordless phones, which are actually radios; there are no thought police, but Westinghouse is testing a device that monitors the mental processes of an employee while he works, which will probably be in use before the end of the decade.

Less sophisticated surveillance is already a standard feature of many factories and offices. Supervisors routinely listen in on telephone operators and telemarketers (and their customers). Machines known as station message data recorders (SMDRs) collect "raw" data on employees' telephone habits—whom they call, for how long, at what time of day—which are then analyzed by data analysis firms. Sometimes these analyses reveal a creative side of an employee that his or her work may not. Employers who engage in such practices like to tell the story of the secretary who had been calling her mother long-distance every day to listen to her favorite soap opera. If that sounds too much like Ronald Reagan's pet anecdote about the woman who used her food stamps to buy vodka, it should at least be mentioned that SMDRs uncovered hundreds of thousands of dollars' worth of calls from the Pentagon to dial-porn services during the Reagan administration.

Other kinds of computers are used to keep tabs on their operators, tracking their productivity, their accuracy, the number of breaks they take. The Agriculture Department's National Finance Center, for example, scrutinizes productivity statistics the way baseball managers follow RBIs and ERAs. It issues reports on the number of entries, the number of errors, the number of trips to the rest room made by data transcribers daily, weekly, and monthly. The data transcribers are not alone. Some 6 million Americans have their work overseen by computers. An even larger number have their telephone calls monitored.

Computers, of course, cannot tell why a certain word processor has a fifteen-minute surge of Olympic vitality after every ten-minute trip to the bathroom. To find that out, employers have drug tests. This year they will spend about $160 million on urinalysis kits alone. The trouble is that the tests are not exactly accurate. Not only can't they pinpoint when the drugs were taken—whether it was on the weekend or during working hours—they can't always distinguish between the licit and illicit, between herbal tea and marijuana. Not to worry. A more precise instrument, the Veritas 100 Analyzer, has recently come onto the market. According to the manufacturer, it can tell if a person is on drugs or alcohol by examining the corneal-retinal potential transmitted along the vestibular nerve—that is, by looking at certain brain waves. They claim that it is accurate 99 percent of the time.

The Veritas 100, which is used both by police departments and personnel departments, displays, prints, and stores each test result. What happens to the record after that is a matter of conjecture, but there is a better than good chance that it will wend its way into an employee dossier, an insurance file, and perhaps one of the country's eighty-five computerized law-enforcement data banks, where it will be added to the 300 million or so records the government holds on more than 114 million individuals. These numbers are swelling like the fat cells of a chocoholic. But unlike the chocoholic, whose waistline is also expanding, the record-keeping systems in which the files are kept are becoming more trim. A computer that filled a whole room forty years ago is today the size of a paper clip, and now the room is filled with computers. According to the Office of Management and Budget, the federal government has a million computers. Thirty years ago it had about a thousand. But that was before the dawn of the information age, which, it turns out, has little to do with knowledge and everything to do with the collection, storage, and sale of data. Whereas half the population in the late nineteenth century worked in agriculture, one hundred years later half the population harvests mailing lists, tax preparation software, silicon chips, and credit histories. And the number of companies that manufacture and sell computer and communication services is growing faster than the overall gross national product.

Now, due to advances in communications technology, computers can talk to one another, which generates still more information, still more markets. Thankfully, their ability to converse makes a centralized, national data bank unnecessary. But it means instead that a decentralized national data bank already exists. "It is technically feasible to have an interconnected electronic network of federal criminal justice, other civil and perhaps even military record systems that would monitor many individual transactions with the federal government and be the equivalent of a national data base surveillance system," the Office of Technology Assessment reported to Congress in 1985. One year later (about seven years later in computer years, given the brevity of computer generations) it revised its opinion: ". . . the widespread use of computerized data bases, electronic record searches and matches, and computer networking is leading rapidly to the creation of a *de facto* national data base on most Americans."

In 1977 the federal government undertook its first national computer match, a comparison of the welfare rolls with federal payrolls, in an effort to catch double-dipping federal employees. Since then, the government has used computers in this way to flush out cheats and delinquents: Aid to Families with Dependent Children (AFDC) payments are matched against Social Security Administration earnings records, tax records against selective service records, motor vehicle records against draft registration records, Veterans Administration records against supplemental security income records.

One search that does not appear to have been made, however, is the one that compares the number of computer matches made last year with the number this year. "It is difficult to determine how much computer matching is being done by federal agencies, for what purposes, and with what results," the OTA reports. "However, [we estimate] that in the five years from 1980 to 1984, the number of computer matches nearly tripled." Since tripling is not a particularly helpful concept when you don't know the number that is being tripled, the experience of the State of Pennsylvania may be more illustrative. In 1975, two years before the first federal match, it compared state and federal tax returns in order to locate residents who had not paid state tax. Ten years later Pennsylvania was running twenty-six matches and had plans for a dozen more.

While computer matching is a fishing expedition with drift nets, a newer procedure, computer-assisted front-end verification, uses the trawler to blockade the harbor. Say an individual applies for government benefits, a government contract, or a loan. That application is checked against various, discrete record systems such as those maintained by credit bureaus, health insurers, the FBI, and the Internal Revenue Service, and it cannot be approved until these systems are cleared. In other words, computer-assisted front-end verification presumes guilt until innocence can be established. Most of the time applicants are not told which government records will be searched, that private-sector records will be looked at, that a profile of the applicant may be drawn from such diverse sources as the National Drivers Register, the IRS master file, and the Veterans Administration, and that the sketch may be based on erroneous information.

While it's impossible to know how wrong this information may be, consider this: A few years ago, the

State of Massachusetts decided to match the names of welfare recipients against bank account holdings. The idea was that people with too much money in the bank would be dropped from public assistance. Of 160 people found by the match to be ineligible for benefits and scheduled to lose them, 110 were based on mistaken information—the account numbers were wrong, the social security numbers were wrong, the money was being held in trust for burial expenses. More recently Milwaukee County, which requires the children of families on welfare to attend school, dropped hundreds of families from the welfare rolls based on computerized attendance lists that were found to be 80 percent wrong. Human error and human capacities used to be the brake on our bureaucratic drives. Files were scattered, they were out of place, they were piled too deep to negotiate. These days errors surface long enough to deny someone Medicare benefits or flag a tax return for an audit. It is all so mysterious, so murky, except for the consequences.

A number of years ago Frank Church, chairman of the Senate Intelligence Committee, warned Congress that "[i]f this government ever became a tyranny, if a dictator ever took charge in this country, the technological capacity that the intelligence community has given the government could enable it to impose a total tyranny and there would be no way to fight back. . . ." As terrifying a prospect as this is, it's only viscerally terrifying, the way earthquakes are when you're visiting San Francisco. The fact is, a change from government by the people to government by one person, or from a government predicated on liberty to one mired in control, may be incremental rather than cataclysmic. The evolution may be so evolutionary, the mutation so apparently natural, that we won't notice.

One hundred years before Orwell wrote *1984*, Alexis de Tocqueville, speculating on the future of American democracy, wrote: ". . . I think that the type of oppression which threatens democracies is different from anything there has ever been in the world before. . . . In the first place, I see an innumerable multitude of men, alike and equal, constantly circling around in pursuit of the petty and banal pleasures with which they glut their soul. . . . [The government] covers the whole of social life with a network of petty, complicated rules that are both minute and uniform . . . it does not break men's will, but softens, bends and guides it; it seldom enjoins, but often inhibits action; it does not destroy anything, but prevents much being born; it is not at all tyrannical, but it hinders, restrains, enervates, stifles and stultifies so much that in the end each nation is no more than a flock of timid and hardworking animals with the government as its shepherd."

Although Senator Church may have a more up-to-date knowledge of the technology, Tocqueville may have a better grasp of its potential. Our bureaucratic impulses—departments of this small thing and that, their insatiable appetite for raw data—act as viruses traveling through the body politic, weakening it. "People do indeed protest what they consider 'unfair surveillance,' often in the same breath with which they demand more vigorous surveillance for purposes they support," observes Professor James Rule of the State University of New York. And, he notes, "people seek their own just deserts, in terms of the credit privileges, insurance rates, tax liability, passport use, or whatever, to which they feel themselves entitled. At the same time, the public also demands effective discriminations against welfare cheaters, poor credit risks, dangerous drivers, tax evaders, criminals, and the like."

The 1990 Louis Harris survey, "Consumers in the Information Age," commissioned by Equifax, the international credit bureau, bears this out. While a sizable majority, 76 percent, said it was not acceptable for credit bureaus to supply direct marketers with lists of people who appeared to be good credit risks so the marketing companies could target them for solicitations, most of them changed their minds when the question was reworded to reflect "a more balanced description of direct marketing." On the second time around, participants were told: "Increasingly, companies are marketing goods and services directly to people by mail. Some reasons for this trend are that many people have less time to shop or they prefer to make shopping decisions at home. Also, companies are trying to reduce their costs of advertising and selling in stores, and they find direct marketing can reduce their expenses and their product prices. Companies try to learn which individuals and households would be the most likely buyers of their products or service. They buy names and addresses of people in certain age groups [and] estimated income groups . . . so they can mail information to the people they think will be most interested in what they are selling." By the time participants got around to being asked if they found this practice acceptable, 67 percent said they did.

What this fickleness suggests is that people are at least as protective of their status as consumers as they are of their privacy. What they seem not to realize, until the telemarketer calls during dinner *again*, is that consumerism and privacy are essentially incompatible, that the one diminishes the other. For example, without submitting to credit checks, people would not be able to have credit cards; without credit cards, people would not be able to buy the things they want without having the money to pay for them. Just over half of the respondents to the Harris survey said they were "very or somewhat upset" about the amount of debt they carry, but 78 percent said they would be upset if they could not obtain credit based on their record of paying bills, and 71 percent believe that consumers have lost all control over how companies use personal information. (And this was before Equifax culled its credit files to supply the names, addresses, income brackets, product preferences, and other personal data on 120 million consumers to the Lotus Development Corporation, which was planning to put this information on computer disks and sell it to anyone who wanted to use it to fashion his own mailing list. ("It must be good—the American Civil Liberties Union already says it raises 'serious legal and ethical questions,' " said a squib in *Advertising Age* about "Lotus Marketplace: Households.") The project was eventually abandoned, after Computer Professionals for Social Responsibility issued a call to action over electronic bulletin boards and 30,000 letters of inquiry and complaint were sent to the software company.

Appearing on mailing lists and receiving telephone solicitations—both consequences, it seems, of buying *anything*—are inconveniences, but only minor inconveniences. Still, they soften the border, so when the government steps over it and starts buying direct marketing lists to determine which purchasers of gas grills and Porsches are short-changing the tax collector, we hardly pay attention. Silence can be interpreted as tacit consent. The state imagined by Tocqueville slowly comes to be.

But the state is only part of it, the obvious part— and weren't we raised by John Locke and Thomas Paine and George Orwell and Richard Nixon to be suspicious of government? It's not only the FBI who is reading our mail and peeking into our bedrooms, not only the IRS tapping the company phone. It's husbands snooping on their wives and business executives spying on the competition; it's computer hackers; it's purchasers of the Listenaider, a device, sold through upscale mail-order catalogs, that enables you to hear other people's conversations; it's the neighbors who tip the credit bureau about the habits of the man next door; and it's women who hire private investigators to check out prospective suitors, to make sure they are who they say they are, to make sure they are free of sexually transmitted diseases, to make sure they are truly eligible bachelors. ("People want to find a quality partner," an investigator who does this sort of work told a *New York Times* reporter. "They don't want to make a mistake that's going to cost them years and a lot of money.")

In the story of Isaiah, God chastises the Israelites for trusting the horses and chariots of the Egyptians instead of trusting Him. Nowadays most of us might trust the chariots (especially if they were made in Japan), but only a few are acquainted enough with horses to trust them, and even fewer still are acquainted with God. Even so, it is clear that trusting God is the basis of religious faith.

Similarly, trusting each other is the beginning of a certain secular faith, a faith that allows us to live in families and communities and nations. Democracy, above all other forms of government, requires this faith—without it there could be no free speech, no free elections, no assumption that today's legislative minority will form part of tomorrow's legislative majority. "God makes us . . . capable of liking virtue before we possess it," the Trappist monk Thomas Merton says. Trust, which is a virtue, is also a habit, like prayer. It requires exercise. And just as no one can run five miles a day and cede the cardiovascular effects to someone else, no one can trust for us. Forgetting how to trust, we rely on random drug tests, honesty examinations, telephone monitoring, and credit checks of prospective suitors. Forgetting how to trust, we find ourselves in Ed Sklar's office, deciding between Garfield the Cat and the briefcase tape recorder.

I Spy

LET'S say you just paid off most of your MasterCard balance or sold your house in Atlanta. Let's say you beat your teenager in straight sets and your sister finally dumped her creepy boyfriend. Let's just say that you're feeling pretty good about yourself and the world, and let's say you want to keep it that way. Then forget about getting to know Frank Jones.

Mr. Jones is a chunky, forty-sevenish man with a mustache that would look like a haystack in a painting by Monet if the hay (or the painting) had been left out in the field for a couple of years. He's built as if he might have played football but then decided, hey, I can kick back and watch it on the tube and drink a couple of beers and never worry about not coming off the bench. He's probably not the sort of guy you'd want to say this to directly.

Frank Jones is a cop. That's not the whole truth, since he left the payroll of the New York City Police Department fourteen years ago, but he's got the bluff and swagger of a cop: he can make you feel you're committing larceny when you take a few breaths in his presence. Nowadays he is one of Ed Sklar's competitors in the surveillance equipment business. Or, as he would have it, Mr. Sklar is one of *his* competitors.

"Guess what Sklar was doing three years ago?" he

challenges me. I say I have no idea. "Three years ago he was a frigging hamburger salesman." Mr. Jones produces a piece of paper that seems to indicate that Mr. Sklar used to run a couple of fast-food restaurants, a claim that Sklar will later deny. His own pedigree is on the wall—a massive bas-relief plaque thanking Mr. Jones for service to the Bureau of Alcohol, Tobacco and Firearms, where he spent a year on loan from the NYPD. The wall is in his office in the back room of his new store, The Spy Shop, a retail outlet for merchandise he had been selling by mail out of New Jersey. When I ask him how business is, he asks me what kind of car I think he drives. I say I have no idea. He tells me I never will.

If Mr. Jones sounds angry when he says this, it's because he's the type of guy who has no truck with people who aren't as smart as he—unless they are paying him. How much would that be? It's hard to say. Mr. Jones, in addition to selling surveillance and countersurveillance equipment, is able to go out into the field and use it: He's a licensed private investigator. He works on a sliding scale.

"You drive up in a Mercedes, I charge you one thing," he explains. "You come in one of those Japanese jobs, I charge you something else." He will, though, let you get away with paying him a minimum of two thousand dollars a week for his services.

One of the things Mr. Jones will do for you in that week is check your office environment—your fans, lamps, light switches, heating ducts, computers, pen and pencil sets—for bugs. I know this because Mr. Jones publishes a brochure with a picture of a man who looks like Joe Friday calling a man who looks like Clark Kent, while a man in a black fedora and dark glasses listens in, and the caption, "We keep your private business . . . from becoming public!" on the cover. The text inside is written in antiphonal Greek-chorus style:

How vulnerable are you?
A tap may take place during the few minutes you are away from your desk.

Who'd want to bug me?
The Activist, The Dissident . . . Unions . . .
Dedicated, yet misguided activists may wish to further their own cause by releasing your private disclosures to the media.

What We Do
A comprehensive threat assessment will be made of all designated target areas and a plan developed to best implement the countermeasure sweep.

Obviously we do a great deal more
during a countermeasure inspection than most companies. This, of course, is reflected in our sometimes higher prices.

Mr. Jones shows me his calendar. On it is the name of a prominent New York City politician. Mr. Jones tells me that he's going to sweep this man's office for bugs the next week. He tells me he did the same for former mayor Ed Koch. When I ask if he found any, Mr. Jones shuffles his hand back into the deck and rakes in his chips.

"What do you think?" he asks, leering pleasantly.

While we talk, another person comes into the showroom, which looks like a cross between a jewelry store and an electronics repair shop. The customer is a plump, middle-aged woman in a flouncy red dress and a white cardigan. She looks at a display of $40,000 transmitters the size of thirsty deer ticks but not as if she were going to buy, talks to one of Mr. Jones's associates, and leaves. When she does, Mr. Jones tells me she is a gypsy with a palm-reading business in Greenwich Village and that he's setting her up with "a system." I hesitate to ask what kind. No matter. Mr. Jones's lips are sealed.

He opens them enough, though, to suggest that I may have a tape recorder buried in the blue knapsack that's slung over my shoulder. At this time I don't know enough about Mr. Jones's product line to ask him if his recorder/transmitter detector—which is the size of a pack of cigarettes and vibrates when it picks up the whir of a tape machine—is out of whack. Rather, I say that I don't have a tape recorder with me. He says he doesn't care if I do. I wish silently—to myself (I think)—that I did have a tape recorder, just in case we run into a slight difference of opinion down the line.

However, among the things he said to me about which I believe there can be no dispute were:

"I own you."

"I can find out anything about you. I can tell what kind of person you are."

"I can sit a mile away, in total darkness, and see into your bedroom."

"Why should I be a guy like Willie Sutton who spends his life in jail? There's still plenty of bank robbers around, but they do it with the telephone, instead of a gun."

"All information is available for a price." (At another time I might have dismissed this, but I had just paid a private eye in Boston $300 to pay a private eye somewhere else to pay a computer hacker in California to find the medical records of a friend of a friend who had been hospitalized four years before in New Jersey. Although it probably wouldn't qualify for a Westinghouse Science Talent Search Award, it was an experiment—we had the patient's permission; the idea was to see if I could purchase someone else's confidential records. I could. The information was delivered in seventy-two hours.)

Mr. Jones also tells me how I can find out the balance

in my neighbor's Citibank account. He instructs me first to consult *Polk's North American Bank Directory*, which lists every bank officer in the country, and pick the name of an officer at any Citibank branch except the one where my neighbor has his account. He tells me, second, to call my neighbor's branch (the number is in *Polk's*). Third, he says, I am to say, "Hi, this is Mrs. Culpepper at Branch 25 and I've got a car loan application from your customer, Mr. Smith, who doesn't remember his account number. While you're at it, what's the balance?"

Although I can't imagine doing this, I can imagine Mr. Jones doing this, especially when he tells me he can find out the balance in *my* bank account and the rest of my financial history with what little he knows about me already: my name, whom I work for, where I went to college. Be my guest, I say, and let me know what you find, since if you find anything, you'll know how to find me. Apparently Mr. Jones likes science as much as I do, because he agrees. Then he cautions me to be careful what I say on the telephone for the next two weeks since you never know who's listening. And, he says as I am leaving to meet my friend Sara for dinner, "Check your clothes. I put a bug on you." I say good-bye to Mr. Jones but make it clear that it's not really good-bye, since we'll be talking again real soon.

In the restaurant I tell Sara about Frank Jones and

the bug he has planted and make her sweep my jacket and knapsack. Like me, she can't find anything that looks like it might cost $40,000. I can tell she is more interested in talking about her contact lens problem than about the fact that Frank Jones is listening to her tell me about it, but she makes a grand gesture of friendship anyway. She takes my jacket out of my hands, holds it up, says, " 'Bye, Frank," into the collar, and gives it back to me. She suggests I park it and my knapsack by the couple next to us who are discussing Sino-Soviet trade relations, which I do. I'm still waiting to hear from Mr. Jones.

23 Hours

Back of Beyond

9 A.M. It is hard to say when the day begins. As Mr. Levine points out, what happens in here bears no relation to what happens out there. In here is the Medical Intensive Care Unit of New York University Hospital, the oldest ICU in New York City, a cramped, febrile room where ten critically ill people lie side by side as intimates, all their living and dying done out in the open. In here the lights never go out and the noise, pneumatic and secular, of the breathing machines, the heart monitors, the blood pressure and respirator alarms, of the people lying down and the ones who stand over them, stops only in the particular, for death. Mr. Levine has been a patient in here for three weeks. He's seventy-four, with a crummy heart. In an ICU, as in certain other bad neighborhoods, words don't necessarily mean what they mean elsewhere and, in fact, may mean their opposite. A crummy heart is a good heart, for example, because it still basically works, and Mr. Levine is on what is known as a Dobutamine holiday, meaning that he can't leave the ICU. Dobutamine, the drug which keeps his heart beating regularly and his lungs fully oxygenated, can be administered only here. While he's on this holiday, Mr. Levine, tethered to his intravenous drip, can sit

up and read a book. Or he can watch the traffic braiding up and down the FDR Drive fifteen stories below, a spectator to "out there." Mr. Levine has one of only two enclosed beds in the unit—a little peace, at least, even if three of the walls are transparent. But don't talk to him about being lucky. No one is lucky in the ICU, he'll tell you, or everyone is, so it is the same thing. Take Dana Morton, in the other isolation bed. A man below the hips, a full-breasted woman above, with a lesion in her brain and left-side paralysis, dying of AIDS. "We love you, Daddy," says a card taped to the wall. Is she lucky to be here, lucky to be alive?

10 A.M. The Critical Care Team—two attending physicians and the three resident physicians they are teaching—pauses on rounds in front of John Mazzelli's bed. Mr. Mazzelli is across the hall from Mr. Levine in the six-bed Coronary Care Unit. Again the nomenclature confuses. There are more patients with diseased hearts in the MICU today than in the CCU, which serves as the intensive care annex. The CCU, however, is, as New York City real-estate agents like to say, a better space: someone thought to erect glass walls between the beds. In every other way, though, the CCU and MICU are indistinguishable.

Dr. Brian Skelly, a young physician who has been awake since sometime yesterday, presents the case. "Mr. Mazzelli is an eighty-eight-year-old man who was admitted with pneumonia. He's got an air leak in his lungs, sepsis, and severe heart failure. He was holding his own until three days ago, when he dropped his blood pressure and his heart arrested. We gave him drugs and CPR. The family refuses to let us put a shunt in his head to relieve the fluid buildup on his brain. They want us to be noninvasive."

As Dr. Skelly speaks, Mr. Mazzelli lies on his back, his head propped to a 45-degree angle. With tubes running from his hands and arms to stands of IV bags on either side of the bed, and a line running into his heart, and three hoses taped to his mouth and nose that cause his chest to rise and fall and rise and fall, he looks like a marionette—but one that has been bound and gagged. He is a tall man, with large, rugged hands and pale blue panicky eyes. He cannot speak, of course, and the doctors think he may be partially deaf, with baseline dementia, a theory they seem to be testing by discussing him as if he weren't there.

"Believe it or not, Mr. Mazzelli's got one of the best prognoses in the unit," Dr. Skelly says.

"Which tells you more about his neighbors than about him," says another resident, Ari Yigdal.

Scanning the other beds confirms this. John Mazzelli's nearest neighbor, Greg Carter, thirty-five, is in an AIDS-related coma. Catercorner to him, Lila Reyes, fifty-two, is paralyzed from the neck down with Guillain-Barre syndrome. Next to her, Janet Wolfson, seventy-eight, has multiple organ failures, while in the cubicle next to Mrs. Wolfson's, a machine is forcing Jack Stoner's moribund forty-three-year-old heart to beat. Mr. Mazzelli may well be the healthiest of the lot. He is also the oldest in the CCU. This is unusual, not because he is so old but because the others, in ICU terms, are so young. Across the hall, for instance, Mr. Levine, at seventy-four, is a stripling; the majority of his bedfellows are ten or twenty years older than he. (Except for AIDS patients, truly young people are more likely to wind up in the hospital's trauma unit or in its surgical, neurological, or pediatric intensive care units because of the kinds of injuries and illnesses to which they are prone.) At University Hospital the medical intensive care unit and the CCU seem to be reserved for people who would be near the end of their lives even if they weren't sick.

11 A.M. "Let's talk about Mr. Robbins," says Carl Kirton, the head nurse, to the social worker, the patient representative, and the pastoral care student, who are making their daily pass through the unit. Mr. Robbins, who is ninety-one, entered the hospital with broken ribs and later developed pneumonia. He has been in the hospital for six weeks, unable to shake the pneumonia, and now he is barely conscious, unable to breathe without mechanical assistance, and his blood pressure has been dropping precipitously. His breast-

bone is bowed from scoliosis, his arms and legs have
withered. The doctors say he is uncommunicative,
that he doesn't make eye contact when they ask him
to or squeeze their hands on command. His oldest
daughter, Jill, says this is because he is furious with
the doctors for what they have done to him. She says
that when she asks him to blink or press her fingers,
he does.

It is the daughter, a divorced, middle-aged
woman, whom everyone on the social service team
really wants to talk about. The doctors have asked her
to consider approving a Do Not Resuscitate Order
(DNR) for her father, her only living parent. They
believe they have done everything possible for him
medically and that he might linger for weeks or months
in the condition he is in, with no chance of recovery.
A DNR allows the hospital staff to stand by and do
nothing when a patient goes into cardiac arrest or
respiratory failure. It is a way, after hooking a patient
up to all the engines of modern medicine, to let him
run out of steam.

Doctors, especially doctors at private hospitals, do
not write DNRs easily, for they admit a certain kind
of defeat. As Dr. Brian Kaufman, the head of the
critical care team treating Mr. Robbins, says, "Doctors
feel uncomfortable not doing therapy." By way of illustration he relates the story of a woman he was treating at Bellevue Hospital who had AIDS. "She was

hypoxic," he says. "Not enough oxygen to her brain. She said she didn't want to be placed on a respirator. Can you say she was competent? No. We put her on a respirator."

The law of informed consent—which began to develop around the time anesthesia was introduced and patients, rendered senseless, with no capacity to control what happened to their bodies, woke up with legs and breasts missing—demands that doctors discuss treatment options with their patients and obtain their approval before they proceed. "Every human being of adult years and sound mind has a right to determine what shall be done with his own body; and a surgeon who performs an operation without his patient's consent commits an assault, for which he is liable," Justice Cardozo wrote in 1914 while on the New York Court of Appeals. But Martin Robbins is not of sound mind, or so his doctors say, so they must turn to his closest relative, his daughter, Jill, to get her blessing for what they want to do.

The problem is that Jill Robbins does not want to make this decision. She wants her father to. She thinks his mind is perfectly sound. But when she tells him what the doctors are recommending and asks him what he would like them to do, she says his hand goes slack in hers. She takes this to be a sign that he does not want to make this decision either. Until he gives her some guidance, she doesn't feel comfortable taking a step that is more than likely to result in his death. In the meantime she wants the medical staff to continue treating her father's illnesses aggressively, a desire they are familiar with and cannot, in this case, wholly abide. "We never do *everything*; we always use medical judgment," Dr. Kaufman says. "What's the limit? It's purely arbitrary on our part. We are not going to do things that are medically futile." He says that if Mr. Robbins goes into cardiac arrest, the doctors will do CPR but "a short one."

Jill Robbins is convinced that the doctors and the nurses and the social service staff want her to sign the DNR because they need the bed her father is in. She also believes that because NYU is a teaching hospital, her father is being practiced on, a fear that is probably not altogether unfounded. In a few hours, for instance, an intern will ask a medical student if he's ever put an arterial line into a patient, and he will supervise the student as he passes a needle through the skin on Mr. Mazzelli's right hand and threads a tube into his artery. For the moment, though, the social service team is convinced Jill Robbins is misconstruing everything that is said to her and everything that is done. The doctors think she is under such terrific stress that she is no longer completely rational. She has asked to see a priest, and one is scheduled to see her today.

"Stay tuned," Carl says, moving on.

NOON. No one delivers bowls of broth or vanilla pudding, no one comes around with anything that resembles what might have come out of a kitchen—there are only nurses hanging nutrition bags filled with milky, viscous formula above the beds, and gravity, and tubes that act as sluices into the nose or the chest or the arm. Lunch and dinner and breakfast are as meaningless here as night and day. That is, until someone asks that the feeding tubes be disconnected. Then breakfast, lunch, and dinner are the difference between day and night.

It is December 5. Tomorrow will be a year to the day that the parents of Nancy Beth Cruzan asked the Supreme Court to allow them to disconnect the feeding tube that doctors surgically implanted when it was unclear what would be the outcome of the car accident that left their twenty-five-year-old daughter dead in a ditch for fifteen minutes before paramedics restarted her heart. That was seven years ago, and now they know. Her brain is profoundly and irreversibly damaged, she is incontinent and subject to seizures, and her limbs are so twisted that her fingernails dig into her wrists. The clinical term for her condition is persistent vegetative state, and her doctors say that as long as she is fed by tube, the thirty-three-year-old woman could endure for another thirty or forty years. Her parents believe that she wouldn't want to live like this. The State of Missouri, where they are from, says that while they may be right, the Cruzans don't have enough evidence to back it up, and that in the absence of such evidence the state has an overriding duty to preserve and protect life.

"The difficulty with the petitioners' claim is that in a sense it begs the question," Justice Rehnquist wrote for the majority in its decision, issued in June 1990. "[A]n incompetent person is not able to make an informed and voluntary choice to exercise a hypothetical right to refuse treatment or any other right. Such a 'right' must be exercised for her, if at all, by some sort of surrogate. Here, Missouri has in effect recognized that under certain circumstances a surrogate may act for the patient in electing to have hydration and nutrition withdrawn in such a way as to cause death, but it has established a procedural safeguard to assure that the action of the surrogate conforms as best it may to the wishes expressed by the patient while competent. Missouri requires that evidence of the incompetent's wishes as to the withdrawal of treatment be proved by clear and convincing evidence. The question, then, is whether the United States Constitution forbids the establishment of this procedural requirement by the State. We hold that it does not."

But the Supreme Court was itself begging the question asked by Nancy Cruzan's parents. Doesn't the Constitution guarantee the right to die? they demanded. The justices hedged. "This is the first case in which we have been squarely presented with the issue of whether the United States Constitution grants what is in common parlance referred to as a 'right to die,' " Justice Rehnquist wrote. "We follow the judicious counsel of our decision in *Twin City Bank* v. *Nebeker . . .* (*1897*), where we said that in deciding 'a question of such magnitude and importance . . . it is the [better] part of wisdom not to attempt, by any general statement, to cover every possible phase of the subject.' " So the court stuck to the narrow inquiry, addressing whether or not a state can impose stringent evidentiary requirements in cases where patients are too absent to have desires or too incompetent to articulate them, and deciding they could. As for those who are competent, moreover, the justices ceded little ground, allowing only that ". . . *for purposes of this case,* we assume that the United States Constitution would grant a competent person a constitutionally protected right to refuse lifesaving hydration and nutrition." If they understood the Constitution to guarantee a right to die, they weren't saying.

Having won its point, the State of Missouri dropped out of the case. The Cruzans did not. In November they returned to the Jasper County Courthouse in Carthage, Missouri, with three of their daughter's friends, each of whom testified to specific conversations when Nancy said she would never want to end up living "like a vegetable" on life-support machines. The Cruzans will win this round, if winning is what it is to have a court sanction the starvation of your child. In just ten days, on December 15, the court will accept the testimony of Nancy Cruzan's friends. And in three weeks, on the day after Christmas, her body will finally be allowed to catch up to her brain.

But right now, here today, Jack Stoner's respirator alarm is ringing, as is Greg Carter's, and the room is filled with what sounds like busy signals being broadcast over a speaker-phone. You would think it was an emergency, except that none of the nurses look up from what they are doing, and soon enough the alarms turn themselves off. Just as they do, the double doors to the CCU swing open the way they do in television medical dramas, and about seven people rush in, the first two pushing furniture and trash cans aside, the others running a bed with a woman on it into the corner cubicle, the one behind Jack Stoner's.

"Relax, Elaine," one of the nurses calls to the woman on the bed, who is naked under the sheet, as she and the others attach a heart monitor and a Pleur-Evac to drain her lungs and hang her IV bags from metal trees like Christmas ornaments.

A doctor arrives, a blond young woman in a short skirt chewing Juicy Fruit, who is about three times younger than the patient. She tells the woman on the bed that they will try to remove the respirator tomorrow. "You just rest now," the doctor says as a nurse on one side of Elaine Beaton's bed begins to call out numbers to a nurse on the other: "BP 110, PDA

11-14, wedge 9-12, cardiac output 3.5. Sodium pre-op 122. Post-op 122." It sounds like the stock market report, or the payout of the third race at Aqueduct—anything but what it is. What it is is what the doctors like to call a "known complication of surgery"—in the course of operating on her heart the surgeon accidentally poked a hole in Elaine Beaton's right ventricle, so instead of being in the recovery room, here she is in the CCU, and who knows for how long. There is a man in the surgical intensive care unit down the hall who went for a triple bypass and something similar happened to him. That was six weeks ago.

1 P.M. Jack Stoner, the man with the crippled heart, can't see his girl friend or mother, who have come to visit him. They speak directly into his ear as if it were a microphone, telling him the darkness is temporary, that his eyes are bandaged to reduce swelling. Up close like this they don't have to compete with the two metronomes that mark time at the foot of the bed—the breathing machine that sends air into his lungs and the pump that forces blood through the heart that soon may not be his. "The only thing that's wrong with him is fixable," says Dr. Kaufman, when asked why he is keeping alive a man whose main muscle has deteriorated beyond repair. One of the residents treating Mr. Stoner, John Raynor, puts it another way.

"As a doctor, it's hard to face 'terminal' heart disease because there are so many things you can do." For Jack Stoner, though, there is only one thing left—a new heart. Because a hospital a few miles north is a designated transplant center, the doctors at University Hospital are trying to have him transferred there, but his admission into the transplant program is far from certain.

"The rabbi was here and said prayers for you," Mr. Stoner's girl friend, who has yellow curls and a face that could advertise Irish soda crackers, tells him. She recites something in Hebrew, and then in English. "And thou shall love the Lord thy God with all thy heart and all thy soul . . ." she says. Mrs. Stoner holds her son's hand. She has told the social worker she is jealous of the girl friend, who can cry.

A bearded man in an overcoat arrives. The rabbi. He takes over from the girl friend while she and the mother talk with a hospital administrator who has come to ask permission to test Mr. Stoner for HIV disease. The mother will have to agree to the test if she wants her son to be a candidate for transplant surgery.

"We're going to test for AIDS," Dr. Kaufman explains, "not because we discriminate against people with AIDS but because you don't want to waste twenty thousand dollars on someone without an immune system."

This isn't fair, of course—which is to say it is not

egalitarian. It is not fair, either, that hearts and livers and lungs are not distributed on a first-come, first-serve basis, and that the person at the top of the list today may be bumped three places back tomorrow. But fairness will be the death of someone like Jack Stoner, whose heart is so badly damaged that he will die if he can't jump the queue. Medicine is not a democracy. It supplies the evidence that people are not created equal, and in times of crisis it is counted on to act on it.

2 P.M. "Two bells," John Raynor, a first-year resident, says to Jim Adams, an intern, as they pass a bag of Pepperidge Farm Mint Milano cookies back and forth across a desk in the corner near the bathroom. The two doctors have been on duty for six hours; they have twenty-seven hours to go on this shift. Tonight will be their night, as it is every third night, to be on call. They will be in charge of patients, nurses, and the rest of the medical staff in the MICU and the CCU. The doctors are young—neither has yet seen the far side of twenty-eight—and desperately cynical. John Raynor is a rangy midwesterner, Jim Adams, a bow-tied Georgian, too intense to be a good ol' boy, but maybe just too tired.

In the course of their training, Dr. Adams and Dr. Raynor have rotated through University Hospital (where they are now), a private, sophisticated medical center that tends to attract patients who can afford its high-priced and highly prized care; Bellevue Hospital, New York City's most notorious public hospital, the place that television news crews always go when they want footage of people who have spent days in the emergency room waiting for a bed (but known also for the delicate needlework of its microsurgeons); and the Manhattan Veterans Administration Hospital. The three hospitals sit in a row on First Avenue in Manhattan, from 34th Street to 23rd Street, a solid half mile of the most aggressive, and arguably the most advanced, medical care available anywhere. It was at Bellevue, after all, that a group of nineteenth-century society ladies who apparently appreciated the germ theory of disease more than their doctors, organized one of the first schools of nursing in the world. Intensive care is a direct descendant of their efforts. Unlike a regular patient floor, where a single nurse takes care of eight patients, in the ICU the nurse-patient ratio approaches a whole number. One nurse cares for one or two patients. The doctors, too, have fewer patients, about half the load elsewhere in the hospital. This is necessary, given what they have to do. Surveillance is constant. A video camera sweeps the room, catching patients unaware in their bed. Social workers keep tabs on their emotions. Every physical fact of their lives is known, monitored, stored. Respiration, urine output, fluid intake, blood pressure, blood sugar, and blood gases are observed and controlled. For this, money is no object. Modesty, reticence, seclusion—these are unaffordable.

3 P.M. One of the doctors nods toward Greg Carter's cubicle, where two men are visiting along with Carter's mother and sister, and says, "The undertakers are here." Carter is dying of AIDS. His eyes are open and fixed on the ceiling. His mouth is gaping, as if he were trying to say one last word when rigor mortis set in. The family has decided that when his heart fails, he won't be revived. Just today the priest told the family to start thinking about the funeral mass. But the two men at Mr. Carter's bedside are not measuring him for his casket; they are his friends, and one of them is telling Mrs. Carter and her daughter about a five-course chicken dinner he attended where three pieces of white meat and three pieces of dark were placed on every plate. He tells them in detail how the chicken was trussed and how the breast was carved. The mother and daughter ask a number of questions. The man who went to the party answers them avidly. The other man says nothing. It is possible that this is the way the one in the bed gets a glimpse of what life will be like when he is gone.

4 P.M. An intern who has been on duty since eight o'clock yesterday morning reports to Dr. Adams on his way out.

"Mrs. Beaton, eighty-two, puncture in right ventricle. Mr. Carter, thirty-five, he's DNR and occasionally has seizures. Mrs. Wolfson, seventy-eight-year-old black woman with diabetes and kidney and heart failure—if you get bored you can extubate her. Mr. Potts, he's being liberated from the vent. He's got a great gas. Mr. Robbins, the cocktail for him is albumen times two. Check his I's and O's. He's precarious . . . like everyone else."

"A fluid nightmare," Dr. Adams says.

"Dana Morton, he/she is alert and quite bitchy," the intern says. The doctors decide not to do a fungal culture on him because they doubt that he will still be alive by the time they get the results from the lab.

"Mr. Mazzelli. He's got cardiomyopathy and sepsis. He needs a new arterial line."

Meanwhile, Dr. Raynor checks on Mrs. Reyes, the woman who is paralyzed. Twenty days ago she could walk, inhale, scratch her head, bend over. Nineteen days ago her fingers became numb, and then her toes, and pretty soon she lost touch with her arms and legs and torso. She's been in the hospital for two weeks, getting progressively worse. "Increase the pain medication," Dr. Raynor says to the nurse. "Thank you, Doctor, thank you very, very much," says the nurse, who normally works on a different floor of the hospital. Her name is Reyes, too, and the patient who cannot move is her mother.

Dr. Adams catches up to Dr. Raynor at Mr. Stoner's

bedside. "No news on his move," Dr. Raynor tells the intern. "His crit is twenty-five. Let's give him some blood." They move on.

"Hello," Dr. Raynor says to Mrs. Beaton. "You did fine in surgery. How are you? Can you look at my eyes? Good."

5 P.M. Mrs. Davis, in the bed next to Mr. Robbins, is dead. She was DNR, so no bells rang, and no one can say for sure what time she died. She's still between the sheets, which are wet at the lap, but no one bothers to change them now.

Back in the CCU a nurse suctions Mr. Mazzelli, passing a tube into the ventilator hose to draw out fluid. It sounds just like what it is, someone sipping on a giant straw at the bottom of a giant glass that is not quite empty. As the nurse works on John Mazzelli's lungs, Dr. Adams supervises Dave Preston, a third-year medical student as he attempts to thread a line into one of Mr. Mazzelli's arteries. Leaning over him like this, the three of them look like the pit crew at a road race. The student makes the stick on his first try. It is not clear if the patient appreciates this. He is twitching, with tears in his eyes, and trying to raise his left hand to his face, but his left arm is a tangle of intravenous lines and adhesive tape; he can hardly move it, but he does, and the medical student pulls on it like a lever and prys it down to the bed.

"We're very invasive with these people and some-times we forget to include them," Dr. Adams says later. "They have no context. We haven't known them outside the ICU. It's real difficult to keep them in perspective as people." Without meaning to, the intern hits upon modern medicine's greatest failing—its tendency to view people as bodies, and bodies as con-tainers of data, and to treat the data and not the person—though he doesn't phrase it this way himself. What he does say is: "In this place you can do whatever you want to people. It's like dog lab."

6 P.M. Adele Marshall, the new patient on Mr. Rob-bins's left side who has taken the place of the woman who died makes it easier. She is alert and she can talk—she is alive—and the doctors love her for it.

"How do you feel?" Dr. Raynor asks her. Her heart is in trouble; she's scheduled for bypass surgery in the morning.

"A little uncomfortable in the chest," she says.

"Rest," he tells her.

"Thank you," she says. "Thank you for stopping by."

On Mr. Robbins's right side a nurse is spooning orange Jell-O into Arnold Irving's mouth. This is taken as a sign that he is too well for the ICU. The doctors are looking for signs. They have just received word that there is an elderly man in heart failure on his way to the fifteenth floor. They need a bed. Mr. Irving, whose last intravenous drip was removed just four hours ago, has to go.

7 P.M. Dr. Adams's beeper goes off. Nothing unusual. He answers the page. It is the unit receptionist calling. Someone has left a package for him at the front desk. It is a gift from a patient on another floor who has shed two hundred of the six hundred pounds he carried with him into the hospital. Dr. Adams retrieves the package, a yellow manila envelope, and opens it. Inside is a white tablecloth with scalloped edges. Jim Adams looks at it as if he had never seen a tablecloth before, and is not quite sure what it is, but he is also, obviously, touched. "He said he wants to give me something," he says. "This is something."

Before his beeper went off, Dr. Adams was on his way to the man with one of the best prognoses in the house, John Mazzelli, to put a new intravenous line in his hand. Lines need to be changed every few days to reduce the risk of infection, and it is a rare day when an ICU patient doesn't get at least one new one. This is John Mazzelli's second line change today.

"All right, sir," Dr. Adams says after the needle has gone in one side of the vein and out the other and the vein has collapsed, "you're going to feel another stick." He pushes the needle in again and misses. Apologizing, he tries again. And misses. And again.

And misses. He is no longer talking to the patient. Mr. Mazzelli's eyes glisten. He looks terrified. Dr. Adams palpates the skin, searching for a workable vein. He thinks he has one, and then it gets away.

Across the hall Adele Marshall is calling for someone to bring her a bucket. One of the nurses rushes over and holds it under her chin, and as she does, she and Jill Robbins, who is visiting her father, keep bumping into each other—there isn't room for both of them. On the other side of Mr. Robbins's bed, three nurses are prepping Mr. Irving for his departure. No room there either. Mr. Levine, in his cubicle, reading a thriller, is being weaned from the Dobutamine, though he doesn't know it. Around the corner in the tenth bed, Mrs. Richardson's son, a physician at the hospital, adjusts her nasogastric feeding tube; she had a bedside tracheotomy this morning. This afternoon she wrote, "I'm so bored," on a piece of paper. Mr. Wolfson, sitting at the foot of his wife's bed, fiddles with a piece of red ribbon, absently tying it into a bow.

8 P.M. Twenty minutes into the hour Mrs. Wolfson's heart stops. Nurses, doctors, and students converge by her bed in a matter of seconds, called by a high-pitched whistle only they can hear. They rush by Mr. Wolfson, standing in the hall, gripping his knees, sobbing.

"One and two and three and four and . . ." a nurse

calls out to the medical student, Dave Preston, who is pumping Mrs. Wolfson's chest.

"We've got a rhythm," someone calls out.

"Do we have a pulse?" Dr. Adams says.

They have a pulse.

So far it has been a good night for Dave Preston. He put in an arterial line for the first time and on the first try, and he brought Mrs. Wolfson back to life, something he was unable to do for the five patients he did CPR on before her.

"The good thing about CPR," Dr. Adams says, congratulating Preston, "is that you can't kill them because they are already dead."

9 P.M. Mrs. Wolfson's cubicle drains as quickly as it filled; it was a flash flood, and now it's over, as if it never happened, except to Mr. Wolfson, who is doubled over in the hall, gasping for breath between sobs. Hearts return to their regular persistent rhythms. Dave Preston points out Mrs. Wolfson's on the monitor at the nurse's station. It is a child's drawing of the Alps or the Rockies, all peaks and valleys. To the untrained eye this looks seismic, as if the heart were a fault and the skeleton were tectonic. Preston allows that his eyes are untrained, too. He is only two years out of college. Still, he is arrogant, the way those with limber joints and riparian arteries tend to be. "Personally," he says, "I wouldn't want this. What we do to them . . .

Personally, I don't have any problem letting a person die."

In the literature of medical ethics, a distinction is often made between life and quality of life, and typically the discussion is about what makes life worth living. The ability to think, to act, to be aware, and to love are among the capacities thought to distinguish living from mere heart-beating. For many of the patients here, though, the debate is moot. They can't talk, they can't think straight, they can't think, and the question no longer is about living but about dying. Death with dignity ceases to be a cliché when the flesh becomes a battlefield and the soldiers have no reverence for the land.

Nothing in our secular philosophies prepares us for this. Bentham's utilitarian calculus, the greatest good for the greatest number, doesn't apply. Kant's categorical imperative to universalize our actions doesn't work either. "I ought never to act except in such a way that I can also will that my maxim should become a universal law," Kant says. "Personally, I wouldn't want this," Dave Preston says. And then there is Mr. Wolfson, weeping in the hall.

10 P.M. Mr. Irving is gone and his slot is empty. The man who was supposed to take his place stalled and was towed to the surgical intensive care unit, which

is a few hundred feet from the MICU and that much closer to the elevator.

"He arrested while we were downstairs waiting for the elevator," an intern tells Jim Adams. "We rode up to the fifteenth floor sitting on top of him, pounding the hell out of his chest. It was like something out of *Doogie Howser, M.D.*"

"Or Bellevue," Dr. Adams says.

Once they got his heart beating again, a cardiologist inserted a balloon pump to keep it going, and because the balloon and the heart were too fragile to withstand the trip down the hall, the seventy-six-year-old patient, David Pauley, was parked in the SICU next to a woman with wildly matted hair wearing an oxygen mask, whose arms were suspended in front of her in fishnet stockings. Not that Mr. Pauley has noticed— or can. "He's not really alive," Dr. Adams says. "His heart was pumping at six percent of its capacity. His brain is damaged from the lack of oxygen. We're plotting his demise."

But no one is able to say why he wasn't allowed to die when his heart stopped, why they were determined to beat the life back into him. One of the doctors says something about doing this for his wife, so she can see him before he dies. What she will see is this: her unconscious husband lying naked on top of sheets stained with blood; a crater in his chest where the ribs were broken during CPR; her husband jumping up every time the balloon inflates, like one of those toy spiders attached to a tiny hand pump. She will see that death is the only taboo in the ICU.

11 P.M. "Come on, sweet pea, relax," a nurse yells to the new patient, just up from surgery, who has awakened to find a hose down her throat.

"This lady is driving me nuts," the nurse announces. "Stop it. Stop it."

The woman in the bed is agitated and flailing and gurgling and trying to pull out the tube.

"I need another pair of hands!" the nurse yells. "Another pair of hands!" Two nurses rush over. Together they tie the woman's hands and arms to the metal bars alongside her bed.

"Do you hear me, do you hear me, you're fine," the first nurse says to the woman in the bed. Actually, she yells this, as if the woman, because she has been made dumb, has been made deaf, too.

"You want me to take the tube out for a minute so you can tell me something?" the nurse asks.

The woman nods.

"I told you before that I can't do that," the nurse tells her. "I told you, the tube will come out in the morning."

Two beds down, Adele Marshall has had no choice but to listen to this. "It's so noisy in here," she tells Dr. Raynor, "but I guess that's because it's a hospital."

"You've got a great attitude," John says.

"Get some sleep," a nurse calls to Mr. Potts over in bed seven, who is rattling a Dixie cup filled with coins to get her attention. "Get some sleep because I'm going to be waking you up soon."

MIDNIGHT "For the pious man it is a privilege to die," Abraham Heschel says in *Man Is Not Alone*, and if he is right, Rabbi Greenbaum, in bed 5, is a very privileged man. He is insensible, drifting. His family has hung crepe paper dreidels from the light fixture above his bed. It is almost Hanukkah, almost Christmas. This afternoon the nurses wrapped all the ICU doors with gold, silver, and green foil paper and red velvet ribbons, and now they look like gifts.

Dana Morton, meanwhile, is bleeding. The blood drips down his neck and collects around his collar. When John Raynor sees this, he runs to him, calling for Jim Adams, who sees his friend dive toward the HIV-positive patient hands first, without gloves.

"Don't touch him, don't you touch him, don't you dare touch him!" Jim calls after him, running, too, with a nurse on *his* heels. The three of them huddle around the bed, and when the huddle breaks, they are laughing: the man with the painted toenails is bleeding because he has just been shaved.

1 A.M. David Pauley's wife, children, and her husband's cardiologist sit together in the waiting room.

Except for Mr. Wolfson in the corner, reading the Bible, they are the only ones waiting. The cardiologist tells a joke. "What do you have when you've got a lawyer up to his neck in cement?" he asks. They don't have a clue. "Not enough cement," he says. The son, who might be a lawyer, laughs politely and tells the cardiologist, who might be Jewish, a complicated Jewish joke. The cardiologist laughs and says he'll have to remember it. Mrs. Pauley urges the doctor to lie down on the couch and use her mink stole as a pillow. "Go ahead," she tells him, balling it up, "it's the old one." The doctor, who is wearing blue jeans and a gray athletic sweatshirt, looks tired. He has already left the hospital once tonight thinking the day was over, and now he may be in for a longer haul than he had imagined. "I hate to say this," he told John Raynor a few minutes before he went out to be with the family, "but Pauley is doing better."

2 A.M. "Two bells," John says. The video camera shows Robbins, Wolfson, Potts, Richardson, with a stuffed bear on her pillow, Levine, the rabbi, and the newest patient, doped with morphine, all asleep. It shows a respiratory therapist appearing at Mrs. Beaton's bedside and working on her lungs. It shows a nurse changing one of Jack Stoner's IV bags, John Mazzelli's open eyes, Mrs. Reyes complaining she can't breathe. 2:05: The doctors make Lasix rounds. Lasix is a diuretic commonly given to ICU patients. "Why?" Jim Adams

asks. "Because we control everything. Since we give them a lot of fluid, we want to make sure it comes out again." This reminds him of a joke. "Why does it take four women with PMS to screw in a light bulb?" he asks. "Because it just does!" he shouts. 2:09: Carter's respirator alarm goes off. 2:11: "You say you want Mrs. Reyes to pee, and then you do nothing," one of the nurses complains. Dr. Adams prescribes more Lasix. "It's not enough," the nurse tells him. "Too little is like chasing your tail." They go over to Mrs. Reyes's bedside and check her urine output. "You're such an exhibitionist," the nurse teases Mrs. Reyes, a large woman whose hospital gown has ridden up and over her belly. 2:17: Dr. Adams orders 20 milligrams of Lasix to be introduced through the blue port. He tells another joke. "There are four doctors on a hunting trip. A flock of birds flies overhead, and the radiologist says, 'From their shape they look like ducks, but they may be pigeons, or they could be grouse,' and the birds fly away. A second flock of birds fly over them, and the internist says, 'They look like ducks, but we have to rule out crows, pigeons, and pheasants, first.' The birds fly away. A third flock of birds flies overhead, the surgeon shoots like mad and all the birds fall down dead. He turns to the pathologist and says, 'Which ones are the ducks?'" 2:27: The Lasix seems to be working, but not the catheter. Mrs. Reyes has wet and soiled herself. The nurses discuss eating salt cod as they clean her up. 2:28: Stoner's respirator alarm goes off. 2:30: A nurse suctions Mrs. Beaton. 2:34: Robbins's blood pressure alarm goes off. 2:35: Dr. Adams orders more diuretics for Mazzelli, who is retaining fluid. 2:45: "Our second admission is still alive, unfortunately," John Raynor tells his colleague, "so we are going to have to do some things on him." He is not happy about it. "This is just like any end-stage therapy. If you start nutrition, you can't stop it. If you put in a balloon, you can't take it out." Later he will say to Jim Adams, "Mr. Pauley deserves none of your attention tonight."

3 A.M. I thought I knew what death looked like, but today the idea I had been relying on, that there is a distinction between it and life, no longer makes sense because I've seen Irwin Robbins and David Pauley and Joyce Wolfson and the others who breathe and blink and convert food into fuel, *and then* a nurse comes by and tells the doctors that she's just noticed that Greg Carter has a sine wave, meaning that his heart has stopped beating, and the doctors jump up from what they are doing—entering numbers into a computer— and go and see.

Carter is lying on his back as before, and, as before, his chest inflates and deflates, and his mouth is open and caked with blood that has backed up from his lungs. The blood is as black and thick as boot polish.

Carter's eyes are open. He looks as alive as he did an hour ago. An hour ago you would have said he looked dead. And now he is. Dr. Adams turns off the respirator. He takes the dead man's head between his hands and jerks it to the left and to the right three or four times. He slaps his cheeks. He listens for a pulse and finds none. "I now pronounce you dead," Dr. Adams says. He checks his watch. It is twenty-five minutes after the hour. "Note that the time of death was three twenty-five A.M.," he says out loud.

Dr. Raynor goes to call the family. He wakes Carter's brother, delivers the news, and advises him to go back to sleep and to come to the hospital in the morning. The brother agrees. Dr. Raynor reminds him that it won't be to the fifteenth floor any longer—that he'll find his brother in the morgue.

The next day I see Greg Carter's obituary in the *Times* and am jarred by its simple recitation of facts— the schools attended, the years at the law firm—and it comes as a surprise that he had a life (had gone to work, had worn a suit), and this realization—and that I am surprised by it—is sadder than seeing his body disappear through doors wrapped like Christmas presents. To be honest, that didn't make me sad at all.

4 A.M. The nurses have changed shifts—who knows when—it's only noticeable now that the traffic of resident and attending physicians and students and social

workers and housekeepers and ministers and families has slowed. These nurses are vigilant and talented. They are, for example, able to make a bed with a 195-pound man in it. They work twelve-hour shifts, three days a week. They like the pressure. "Wait, there's something wrong with this picture," one of them says loudly, walking by the two young doctors, who have laid their heads on their desk, buried in their arms, like schoolchildren. "We have people on balloon pumps here!" "Leave them be," another nurse says. But this does not happen. An X-ray technician appears to take pictures of Mrs. Beaton's chest and calls for everyone who can to leave the area. The doctors give up and go down to the cafeteria for coffee and peanut M & Ms.

Except for a few hospital workers the cafeteria is empty, the regulars having gone elsewhere to seek the comfort of darkness. Up in the ICU the lights shine, but the blinds are drawn, and it is a thin veil against what is known as ICU psychosis, a kind of iatrogenic disorder caused not by germs or an errant scalpel but by the place itself, by its days without nights. People can't take it. They go a little crazy. (Torturers know this too. ". . . the worst thing was the loss of time perception, and hope. The cells were artificially lit and the prisoner was called or fed at very irregular intervals. After a while you wouldn't know whether it was day or night, still yesterday or already tomorrow. This unhinged some people," Jorge Valls writes in *Twenty Years and Forty Days: Life in a Cuban Prison*, published by the Americas Watch Committee.)

Dr. Raynor goes off to look in on David Pauley. Jim Adams enters the day's events in the patients' charts. Elaine Beaton's respirator alarm rings, rights itself, rings, rights itself, rings and rings like a telephone on a street corner. A nurse reports that Rabbi Greenbaum's feeding tube is blocked. Dr. Raynor comes back from the SICU. "How is he?" Jim asks, not looking up. "Oh, you know, basically dead," John says.

5 A.M. Katti, a nurse from Denmark who is leaving in a few hours for Copenhagen on a courier flight, stands on a chair in Jack Stoner's room and snaps a few pictures of her buddy, Pam, who is changing one of his IV bags. Katti tells her to smile. The flash triggers. Stoner makes noises like a seal. Pam washes Stoner's face. Katti takes another picture. Pam swabs his teeth. "Open your mouth and stick out your tongue," she tells him. She swabs his tongue. "Thank you. Sorry, Jack. Okay. Let me make the bed. You know what day it is? Today is Thursday, December sixth. The reason it's dark outside is because it's early in the morning. The sun hasn't come up yet." She checks the urine bag hanging off the left side of the bed; his urine is the color of tangerines. "I'm going

to retape this wonderful tube to your nose," she says, and does so. "What is it, sweetheart?" "You cold, Jack?" She pulls a sheet over him. "That's a little better," she says.

6 A.M. This time, when the X-ray technician comes into the unit, the two doctors do not lift their heads from the desk. "I can take a little radiation, as long as I can sleep," Jim says. But he doesn't sleep. John's beeper goes off. SICU rounds are starting. The sun is rising in the southeast, and Katti is taking pictures of the river, which is pink, and the sky, which is, too. Mrs. Beaton's hematocrit level is declining. Mr. Robbins's PO2 is off. John Mazzelli's lungs are swimming. The doctors go off to investigate.

7 A.M. A cardiologist materializes—as doctors, nurses, technicians, and orderlies always seem to be doing in the ICU—and orders more diuretics for John Mazzelli. Dr. Raynor orders transfusions for Jack Stoner and Elaine Beaton. Mr. Robbins gets Lasix; he's retaining fluids, too. The rabbi's eyes are open, his feeding tube is still blocked. Mr. Levine is sitting up in bed, calling for a commode. Mr. Potts is asleep. Mr. Wolfson is by his wife's bedside; her eyes are closed. The timing is off on David Pauley's balloon pump. His cardiologist appears (of course) to fiddle with the knobs. "A balloon can make a difference to people crashing," he says.

"The question is, is there anything here worth salvaging?" The four resident physicians who had the night off wander in, innocent from sleep. They are surprised that Mr. Irving is gone, relieved that Greg Carter died, incredulous that there are two people in the unit at the same time with balloons guiding their hearts.

Jim Adams and John Raynor, who will be on duty for another seven hours, lean against the wall in the corridor between the MICU and CCU, leading morning rounds. "Reyes, uneventful night. Continue with pressure support. She's shrugging her shoulders better. Wolfson, lost pressure last night, less than one minute compression, back to baseline within ten minutes. Stoner, the same. Carter, when the nurse called us he had a sine wave. Mazzelli, he's gotten significantly worse. He's in heart failure. Morton basically had a quiet night. He's awake, he's spiteful—as he probably should be." They continue this way, on down the roster.

"So we have the potential for getting four new patients today," one of the newcomers says when they are finished.

"Or the alternative scenario," says John Raynor. "No one dies. No one moves."

8 A.M. On the street the cold fresh air hits like a revelation, but of what? I once saw a video made by the Mormon Church that showed what it's like after

death, how you meet up with your family in heaven and get along with them there better than you ever did here. I am not enough of a believer to accept that this is how it will be, and I suspect most people aren't either, and maybe this is our undoing. If we were not so sure of ourselves—not just of our capacities and our technologies—but that we are *it* and *this is all*, then death would be a question mark, not a period. "We don't like death any more than you do," Dr. Adams said late last night. "That's what we went to school to stop." They can't, of course. We should be aware of this, and grateful, and if we were, maybe the text of our lives would have what novelists call narrative drive, and we would make our endings integral to the rest of the story.

The newspapers and courts are full of cases like Nancy Beth Cruzan's or Karen Ann Quinlan's, which are obvious and extreme, but the hospitals are full of John Mazzellis and David Pauleys and Janice Wolfsons—our parents, their parents, and ourselves —and these cases are more complicated because they are more common and more mundane. I have heard that at Bellevue people with AIDS are shown the ICU while they are relatively healthy so they can see what it is like to be connected to a mechanical ventilator. Then they are asked to decide if they would want to be intubated. We should all be required to take this tour, and not only for our own sake. John Mazzelli's life is going to end, not with a bang and not with a whimper, and not with fire or ice, but with a hose down his throat and the hiss and rattle of a breathing machine in his ears and an unlimited, unobstructed view of the ceiling. He will wither under the twenty-four-hour grow-lights. It might take a while. This while is what will be referred to as his life.

Solo

WHAT I really want to do is take the dog. We will head off into the woods by the lake; she will be my scout, my guide. She will chase rabbits and flush grouse. I will wade out into the water at noon and float on my back, shielding my eyes to look at her treading water like an otter, barking like a seal. Just after dusk we will sit in the lee of the fire, listening to the bullfrogs grumble, and the owls. When it gets cold I will let her into the tent. I will sleep in *her* lee.

If only I weren't as weak as a new convert, unable to bend the rules. Taking a dog along on a solo camping expedition—isn't that like a hermitage with a telephone? John Burroughs's brief essay on solitude is not yet known to me. "If Thoreau had made friends with a dog to share his bed and board in his retreat by Walden Pond, one would have had more faith in his sincerity," says Burroughs. "The dog would have been the seal and authentication of his retreat." Worried myself about authentication, I take a copy of *Walden* and leave the dog at home.

My husband sees me off. We are a mile down the eastern shore of a lake where our friends' Adirondack guide boat is beached. Hybrid canoe or hybrid rowboat depending on your orientation, a guide boat sits low

to the water on a narrow keel. This one is no more
than six feet bow to stern, with a wingspan, fully
extended, that's maybe twice as long as that. I take
yawning, rangy strokes, going south. In a minute I
turn a bend and lose sight of the landing. I hear the
cough and rattle of our old car as it heads out, and
then I hear it no longer. It is an exquisite summer
day. It's about 78 windless degrees. I am not the only
one out on the lake in a boat, but I am the only one
rowing. I glide past a tree stump, two hundred yards
out, before I see atop it the harbormaster, a great blue
heron, who nods my way with a shiver of feathers.

It is a dogleg lake, three and a half miles top to
bottom, and I am rowing to the spur, where there is
a spit of land shielded by an arc of pines whose soft
brown needles cover the ground. It takes twenty minutes plowing through the water to reach it, and another
twenty to set up the tent. Afterward I open up my
raccoon-and-bear-proof cooler and scrounge around for
lunch. Everything I packed not more than two hours
ago now looks remarkably dull, or worse. Sardines in
tomato sauce? Hard-boiled eggs? What was I thinking?
I settle for apples and cheese and the opportunity to
wield my Swiss army knife like an authentic camper.
I look at my watch. It's 12:17. The day stretches out
before me.

"Sometimes, in a summer morning, having taken
my accustomed bath, I sat in my sunny doorway from

sunrise till noon, rapt in a revery, amidst the pines and hickories and sumachs, in undisturbed solitude and stillness, while the birds sang around or flitted noiseless through the house, until by the sun falling in at my west window, or the noise of some traveller's wagon on the distant highway, I was reminded of the lapse of time," I read in *Walden*. I look at my watch. It is 12:19.

Two fishermen in a Boston whaler make the turn into this part of the lake, cut the motor, and drift. I have chosen this spot to be alone, but not so alone that someone would not eventually hear me if I yelled for help. The edge of the wilderness is not the wilderness, though, and here come my fellow nature lovers to prove it. Propped against a tree, I am not visible, but my tent is, and so is my boat. They know I am here, so I *feel* they can see me, that they are watching. I don't want to be part of their consciousness, part of what they carry away from this scene. I don't want them to know I am here by myself.

All week I have been following the trial of three teenagers who are part of a gang accused of beating and raping a woman who had been jogging through Central Park at night. What was she doing there, people asked each other—didn't she know better? This peculiar distaff knowledge—of the danger of untraveled roads, unpeopled train compartments, empty houses, open fields, and dark streets—stalks women into the woods. Once, 11,000 feet up the side of a mountain, my husband and I stopped to catch our breath at a Park Service hut and read in the visitor's log an entry from a woman who had to stay overnight in bad weather with four men, all strangers. "Spent a fitful night worrying about the one-eyed trouser snake," she wrote the next morning.

In the broad daylight I am not afraid of the fishermen, just annoyed. They have every right to be here, of course, but my annoyance is extrajudicial. "I have my horizon bounded by woods all to myself; a distant view of the railroad where it touches the pond on the one hand, and of the fence which skirts the woodland road on the other. But for the most part it is as solitary where I live as on the prairies," Thoreau writes. I look up and see two men in an outboard, their lines slack, reeling in. I see them cast, port and starboard. Their lures charge toward the water like meteors. I see the men reel in again, snagging a patch of water lilies. I am annoyed because I expected to see something else, some kind of nothing.

Another boat chugs into the bay. I pull myself up and walk deeper into the forest, bushwhacking in as straight a line as possible so as not to get lost, until the water is no longer visible, not even the glint of it. The outboards fade until they're smudges, not fingerprints. I share a log with a colony of termites and a red squirrel that clucks like a bird. "Why does a virtuous man take delight in landscapes?" asks Kuo Hsi, an eleventh-century Chinese watercolor artist in his *Essay on Landscape Painting*. Because "the din of the dusty world and the locked-in-ness of human habitations are what human nature habitually abhors; while, on the contrary, haze, mist, and the haunting spirits of the mountains are what human nature seeks, and yet can rarely find." A plane grinds overhead. It is true that affluence brings solitude and privacy in the form of, for instance, country cottages, cars, and personal aircraft. But only for a minute. Then rural property values increase, houses are built on smaller parcels more closely together, and the highways and airports clog with commuters heading for the hills together. No matter how far I go into the forest today, that plane will still be grinding overhead.

The fishermen retreat a little before five. I follow the throttle and whine of their engines, moving back toward camp as they dim. A wind comes up and passes through the trees on the opposite shore, which rustle in succession like baseball fans doing a wave cheer. The trees are teeming with thrushes. Their voices fill the basin, yet the birds themselves are nowhere seen. So many of our perceptions are learned, not intuitive. I mean, why don't I think the trees are singing?

I shed my shoes and walk into the water, pulling the boat behind me. I know this lake better than I know any other body of water, better than I know the pool of land surrounding my house. I have taken its temperature and measured its pH and acidity; I have swum it side to side, skied its circumference, paddled and rowed it end to end. I have climbed the mountains that grow a few thousand feet above its shore. I have done these things in the gray of winter and at the start of June when the hardwoods hang their damp new leaves out to dry. I have been here at midnight with the beavers, and at dawn with the perch. It is easy to get carried away. "A lake is the landscape's most beautiful and expressive feature. It is earth's eye; looking into which the beholder measures the depth of his own nature. The fluviatile trees next the shore are the slender eyelashes which fringe it, and the wooded hills and cliffs around are its overhanging brows," Thoreau tells us. So easy to get carried away.

Rowing forward, I nose between the remains of what was once the beavers' dinner, many nights running, and is now their leftovers. The lake is so shallow here I can palm the bottom. The warm water rings my wrist like a bracelet. Red-winged blackbirds spy on me and tell the other birds what they see. I am happy—relieved—to be out in the open again. I feel, I think, like a deer at dusk on the last day of hunting season.

. . .

PEOPLE talk about the silence of nature, but of course there is no such thing. What they mean is that *our* voices are still, *our* noises absent. Tonight when my fire failed, I sat on a rock and followed the course of a cloud that looked like a trillium, watching as its whorl broke apart. The frogs were honking like ducks; the ducks were laughing like women. I could barely make them out, those loons, but just before the light faded they rose from the lake, and for a moment their white breasts hung above the water like moons.

In the dark, in the tent, every sound is amplified. Individual mosquitoes demand to be let in. Pine needles fall one by one. A beaver sharpens his teeth on an aspen nearby. Bears on either side of the lake hoot lustily; it is time to mate. I feel safe inside this thin nylon skin, for no apparent reason. So safe, in fact, that once I have drawn in my world between its walls, I grow fearful of what's on the other side. A porcupine screams in the distance. Coyotes bray. The world of night is primal. I am frightened because fear is the only instinct that has not been bred out of me. But the world of night is vast, too. It ignores me. After a few restless hours I fall asleep.

. . .

A MAN wakes me up. He is standing forty feet from my bed in an aluminum boat, baiting a hook. The sun is aloft, barely. He waves to me when I emerge from the tent with the bonhomie of one who has been awake since before dawn. If he wants to chat, I give him no opportunity, abandoning camp for the shore due west where the beavers have carved a rogue obstacle course. Sitting on one of their benches, I notice millions of cobwebs strung from the trees to the water. When the sun shines on them they look like lines of fish wire being pulled in at once. The man in the aluminum boat leaves the neighborhood pursued by a cloud of greasy blue smoke, and I am alone again, and not sure what to do.

If the forest were a room with a door, I'd probably be inside, reading. But the open wood demands something else. A hike up the ridge, an hour with the chickadees—something like that. Solitude would appear to be defined by place as well as dependent upon it. What passes for being alone at home, say, wouldn't pass here. You don't pitch a tent to curl up with a novel.

But this is just an aesthetic. Place is of consequence only to the extent that it encourages or demands the confrontation of the self by the self, which is solitude's true vocation. There is the solitude of experience and the solitude of despair, which can happen anywhere. There is the solitude of the jail cell and of the sickbed and of the hermitage, which differ by degrees of isolation. And there is the solitude of darkness, my grandfather's solitude, which was absolute.

He was fifty-nine when he went blind. Actually, he didn't lose his sight so much as his sight left him, the way a lover might, first in spirit, then in fact. When it was gone for good, friends encouraged him to go to a social service agency, to learn how to be blind. He resisted, memorized the number of footsteps from his apartment to the elevator, from the elevator to the courtyard, from the courtyard to the bus stop. Then, having nowhere to go, he gave in. He was told to report to the Lighthouse for the Blind in Manhattan for aptitude testing.

"My first day there, my wife brought me down from the Bronx, packing a two-sandwich lunch as the cafeteria was under construction," he wrote later, in an essay titled "I Hate Institutions." "After inquiring, we were told where to report, and I found myself in a large noisy room that contained a carpenter's shop, noisy with power machines and noisier semiblind adolescents, and a basket-weaving shop with blind men and women speaking in many different tongues, that to a neophyte like me sounded like the Tower of Babel. The instructor sat me at a bench between a retarded five-year-old blind boy and a man of about twenty-five who did not speak English, while I did not speak his language, so our conversations were held to a minimum. Now my twisting begins, making leather belts, rubber doormats, etc. This method must be all right, but did not appeal to me. When I remonstrated with the supervisor, I was told to be patient and cooperative.

"Then it was time for lunch. I gathered up my sandwiches, which were lying on the bench all morning, and was ushered down to the cafeteria and was left on my own, stumbling, ailing, until I found an empty seat, unwrapped my lunch, and ate the sandwiches in silence, all the time feeling tears welling up in my eyes. I recall having seen such scenes in the movies, and now I was the leading actor and I did not relish the part. Since it only took me fifteen minutes to finish lunch, and having no one to talk to, I wandered out into the vestibule and asked someone to direct me to a phone booth. I called my wife, and as she was asking me about my activities, I broke down and cried. To think that at fifty-nine years of age, having worked all my life, now to face a most difficult future at best. My wife, sensing my disappointment, wanted to come down and take me home, but I warned her off and told her it was a challenge and I was determined to go through with it. This testing went on for five weeks. I kept protesting until I was sent to typing class."

The essay, which was sent to me by a relative who found it when she was cleaning out her desk, is typed.

. . .

I RETURN to what I have begun to think of as my front yard and defiantly open Thoreau. "We need the tonic of wildness," I read, "to wade sometimes in marshes where the bittern and meadow hen lurk, and hear the booming of the snipe." Chastised, I put down the book and survey the great outdoors. An ample, flat-bottomed boat with a blue-and-white-striped awning is steaming into view. Three people lounge on its deck chairs, one wearing a hot pink sweat suit, one in orange-and-blue shorts, the other wrapped head to toe in lemon knit sportswear. This is wildness of a different order. Shortly, a motorized canoe rasps into the inlet behind them, and then come two more canoes, powered by five actual canoeists, who look to be in their sixties. The three women wear fluted bathing suits and have zinc oxide on their noses and shoulders. One of the men wears a Red Sox cap.

My grandfather hated the Red Sox, like any loyal Yankees fan. He adored the Yankees. Even when he couldn't see a thing, he would go to Yankee Stadium and sit there with a transistor radio plugged into his ear, just to cheer. During baseball season, when he came to visit us in Connecticut, he would lie outside in the hot sun, hatless and shirtless, listening to that radio from the first pitch to the last. His scalp would redden, and the sweat would dam on his eyebrows and run into his ears. My mother, his daughter, would try to get him to come inside, or to move under a tree, as if he didn't know exactly what he was doing or where he was. But he knew. Sometimes he would ask me—I was about six—to hold a newspaper in front of his face, and then to take it away, so he could see the light.

. . .

"ARE you going to Denver and then to San Francisco, or are you going through Sacramento?" a woman in one of the canoes asks a man in the other. I don't wait to find out. Vowing to return in a different season, I collapse the tent and stow my gear in the hull of the guide boat, which I pilot past all canoes, paddled and powered, and the floating porch too, rowing home.

A Note on Sources

IN writing this book, I have been guided by a number of authors whose work I admire and cite in the text. These include Emerson ("On Solitude"), Rousseau, *Reveries of a Solitary Walker*, Thoreau (*Walden*), Louis Mumford (*The City in History*), Thomas Merton (*Thoughts in Solitude, The Monastic Journey*), Sissela Bok (*Secrets: On the Ethics of Concealment and Revelation*), and Dietrich Bonhoeffer (*Letters and Papers from Prison*).

Other, unnamed sources have been equally instructive. Alan Westin's *Privacy and Freedom*, written in 1967, remains a definitive and prescient work; *Privacy* (Nomos XIII, 1971), edited by J. Roland Pennock and John W. Chapman, explores the anthropological, legal, sociological, and philosophical angles of privacy in essays by Charles Fried, Edward Shils, John Silber, and others; David Linowes's *Privacy in America*, David Flaherty's *Protecting Privacy in Surveillance Societies*, and Alida Brill's *Nobody's Business: The Paradoxes of Privacy* are among the most current general introductions to the subject; William Faulkner's essay "On Privacy: The American Dream—Whatever Happened to It?" (*Harper's*, July 1955) is perhaps the most trenchant.

Harvard University's *A History of Private Life*, edited by Philippe Aries and Georges Duby, has been invaluable to me and will be to anyone interested in the evolution of domestic living arrangements. So has Witold Rybczynski's *Home: A Short History of an Idea*. Anthony Storr's *Solitude: A Return to the Self* examines the psychological and creative effects of being alone.

The literature on homelessness, AIDS, abortion, and prisons is vast. Among the books which I found especially useful were *Songs from the Alley* by Kathleen Hirsch, *And the Band Played On* by Randy Shilts, *Borrowed Time: An AIDS Memoir* by Paul Monette, *Contested Lives: The Abortion Debate in an American Community* by Faye Ginsburg, and *Prison Memoirs of an Anarchist* by Alexander Berkman.

Although this book is not about privacy rights, it was nonetheless informed by a number of legal documents and law review articles. A century ago, two young lawyers, Samuel Warren and Louis Brandeis, published an article in the *Harvard Law Review* in which they argued that there was, in the common law, a principle, distinct from that which secures private property, that similarly protects the privacy of individuals. The article was seminal; it is where, in American jurisprudence, the right to privacy, and the immense literature it generates, begins. One hundred years later, another young lawyer, Jed Rubenfeld, published a historical companion to the piece by Warren and Brandeis. Like the original, it is called *The Right to Privacy* and was published in the *Harvard Law Review* (February 1989).

I have also relied on a number of government documents. These include the report of the United States Privacy Protection Committee (1977) and various studies commissioned by Congress through its Office of Technology Assessment (OTA): *Electronic Surveillance and Civil Liberties* (1985), *Electronic Record Systems and Individual Privacy* (1986), and *The Electronic Supervisor: New Technology, New Tensions* (1987).

Robert Ellis Smith, a lawyer and writer in Washington, D.C., is an astute, vigilant observer of invasions of privacy by individuals, governments, institutions, and corporations. *Privacy Journal*, which he publishes monthly, is an up-to-the-minute catalogue of his findings. It is frightening, necessary reading.

Acknowledgments

I DIDN'T know Morgan Brown, a Los Angeles AIDS activist, when I called to ask his help in finding a hospice willing to let me stay awhile in order to write about it, but his generosity and kindness were the beginning of a pattern from which this book was fashioned. To him and to the men he put me in touch with, Michael Weinstein, president of the AIDS Health Care Foundation, and Paul Gatto, former director of the Chris Brownlie AIDS Hospice, as well as the residents, staff, and volunteers there, I owe tremendous thanks.

I am also deeply grateful to Patrick Horvath and Doug Lasdon of the Legal Action Center for the Home-

less in New York City; Bob Hayes of the National
Coalition for the Homeless; and Tim Boon, Father Ned
Murphy, Janet Driver (now program director at An-
tonio G. Olivieri Drop-In Center in Manhattan), and
the other residents of POTS House, who opened their
door to me; Dr. Brian Kaufman, for the opportunity
to spend a week with him, the Critical Care Team,
and the house staff in the medical intensive-care unit
at New York University's Tisch Hospital; Dr. Bruce
Lockhart of St. Clare's Hospital in New York; Richard
Hamilton, a private investigator in Boston; and the
Bell family of Indiana, all of whom gave generously
of their time.

Sister Helen Prejean of New Orleans acquainted
me with conditions and inmates at the Louisiana
State Penitentiary. At Great Meadow Prison, my local
guides—Gamel, Warren, and Vincent—asked to be
remembered. Thanks to them and to those who gave
me access to them: Art Leonardo, Janet Gordon, and
Amy Colodny of the New York State Department of
Corrections. At Washington and Moriah Shock Camp
prisons, Keith Kelly and Gary Filion were candid and
giving of their own time and that of their staff
members.

The monks at the Abbey of Our Lady of Gethsemani
took me in. I am grateful to them, especially Father
Felix and Brother Luke.

Gloria Loomis, friend and agent, did countless good

works for me in the course of this project, but it is for the first I am most appreciative. She introduced me to Dan Frank, an incisive, daring, gentle editor. It has been my privilege to work with him.

Many others at Pantheon also aided my efforts, particularly Alan Turkus, Susan DiSesa, Stacey Watt, Fearn Cutler, Grace McVeigh, and Roberto de Vicq de Cumptich. I am also indebted to Kendra Taylor of the Watkins-Loomis Agency.

For her sharp, critical reading of an early draft of this book, and for giving me the opportunity to research and write about some of the issues in it, I am grateful to Barbara Epstein, editor of *The New York Review of Books*.

My friends and family were a constant, reliable source of encouragement and assistance. For my parents, Ted and Bernice Halpern, and my grandmother, Esther Rogoff, for my godchildren Gordie Verhovek and Annie Leary Considine, as well as for Peggy and Gordon McKibben, Peter Halpern, Shawn Leary, Michael Considine, Sam and Lisa Verhovek, David Goldfarb, Lisa Saimon, Jim Hershberg, Patricia Biggers, David Edelstein, Nicky Dawidoff, George Trow, and, especially, Sara Rimer, I am more grateful than I know how to say.

This book is dedicated to Bill McKibben, my husband, partner, and dear friend. His example inspires me. His love sustains me.